Cases of Sherlock Holmes

Cases of

Sherlock Holmes

Sir Arthur Conan Doyle

Adapted by William Kottmeyer
St. Louis Public Schools
Illustrated by Joseph Camana

WEBSTER DIVISION, McGRAW-HILL BOOK COMPANY
St. Louis New York San Francisco Dallas Toronto London Sydney

The Webster Everyreaders

The EVERYREADERS were selected from the great literature of the world and adapted to the needs of today's children. This series retains the flavor of the originals, providing mature content and dramatic plot structure, along with eye appeal designed to motivate reading.

Based upon the original stories entitled "The Speckled Band" and "The Red Headed League" from *The Adventures of Sherlock Holmes* published by Harper & Brothers and "The Adventure of The Six Napoleons" and "The Adventure of The Empty House" from *The Return of Sherlock Holmes* published by Doubleday and Company, Inc. by Sir Arthur Conan Doyle.

Contents

The Adventure of the Speckled Band

I HAVE been working with Sherlock Holmes the past eight years. Today, as I look over my notes I see I have written down over seventy of his detective cases. Some cases were terrible crimes. Some were funny. Many were strange. But every one was an exciting adventure. Sherlock Holmes didn't work to make money. If a case was interesting, he would work on it. If it was not, he would have nothing to do with it.

As I look over my notes, I can't remember a case more strange and exciting than our Speckled Band Adventure. And now at last I may tell the story. The lady in the case died just last month. We had promised to keep her secret as long as she lived.

It was early in April, 1883. I awoke one morning to find Sherlock Holmes fully dressed standing by my bed. I looked at him in surprise. Holmes usually

1

got up very late. The clock said a quarter past seven.

"Sorry to get you up so early, Watson," he said. "But we have work to do."

"At this hour in the morning?"

"Yes. A young lady is downstairs to see me. Mrs. Hudson says she's very much excited. I tell you, Watson, when a young lady runs around London at this hour, something is wrong. She beat on the door and got Mrs. Hudson up. Mrs. Hudson got me up. So here I am to get you. I thought you'd want to get in the case from the beginning."

"I wouldn't miss it."

I jumped into my clothes in a hurry. In a few minutes I was ready to go downstairs. There sat a lady dressed in black. Over her face was a heavy veil. She got up as we came in.

"Good morning," said Holmes. "My name is Sherlock Holmes. This is my friend, Dr. Watson. I have no secrets from him. You can talk freely. Ah, I see Mrs. Hudson has lit a fire. Sit here close to it. I'll get a cup of coffee for you. I see you are shivering."

"I'm not cold," said the woman.

"What's the matter, then?"

"I'm frightened. I'm scared to death." She raised her veil as she spoke. We could see the fear in her eyes. She looked like a hunted animal. Her face

2

looked as though she were about thirty years old. But her hair was gray. She was weary and tired. Sherlock Holmes looked at her keenly.

"Don't be afraid," he said. "Everything is going to be all right. We're going to help you, I'm sure. I see you came in by train."

"Oh, do you know me?"

"No, but I see your return ticket in your glove. You must have started early. You had a long ride over muddy roads before you took the train."

The woman looked at Holmes in surprise.

"There is no mystery about it," he smiled. "The left arm of your coat has seven mud spots. The spots are fresh. Wheels throw mud that way."

"You are right," she said. "I left home before six. I came on the first morning train. I just can't stand this any longer. I'll go crazy unless I get help. I have no one—well, just one. But he can't help me. I've heard of you, Mr. Sherlock Holmes. You once helped a friend of mine, Mrs. Farintosh. I got your address from her. Oh, sir, do you think you could help me, too? Right now I can't pay you. But in a month I'll be married. Then I'll have my own money turned over to me."

Holmes turned to his desk. He pulled out a little black book. He turned the pages.

"Farintosh," he said. "Ah, yes. I remember. That

was before I knew you, Watson. I'll do what I can for you. Don't worry about the money. I work because I like my work. If I have expenses, you may pay them when you can. Now tell us your story so I can help you."

"Oh, it's so hard to make anyone understand. I'm in danger. I know I am. But even the man I am to marry doesn't believe it."

"Go on with your story."

"My name is Helen Stoner. I am also called Helen Roylott. I live with my stepfather, Dr. Roylott. The Roylotts are an old English family."

Holmes nodded his head. "I know the name well," he said.

"The family was once among the richest in England. But they have grown poor through the years. Nothing was left but a few acres of ground and a two-hundred-year-old house. My stepfather's father lived there, poor as could be. My stepfather borrowed some money to go to school. He became a doctor. He went to India, where he did pretty well. But he had a terrible temper. He beat one of his servants almost to death. He had to go to prison for several years. Afterwards he came back to England, a bitter, angry man.

"When Dr. Roylott was in India he married my mother. She was the widow of Major-General Stoner

4

of the British Army. My sister Julia and I were twins. We were only two years old when mother married Dr. Roylott. She had a good bit of money. She had at least a thousand pounds coming in every year. Mother gave all the money to my stepfather. Both Julia and I were to get a part of it when we married. Well, our whole family came back to England. Mother died shortly after we got here. She was killed eight years ago in a railroad accident. When she died, my stepfather left London. He took Julia and me to the old house where his father had lived. We lived on the money mother had left. We had nothing to worry about or to keep us from being happy.

"But my stepfather began to change about this time. He wouldn't make any friends. He would have nothing to do with our neighbors. He shut himself up in the house. Whenever he would come out, he'd have a fight with someone. All the men of the Roylott family have had bad tempers, but he must be the worst. Twice he had to go to court for fighting. Everybody in town is afraid of him. He is a big man and as strong as a giant. When he's angry he'll do anything.

"Last week he threw the blacksmith into the river. I used every cent I could get to keep it quiet. The only people who will have anything to do with him are a band of gypsies. He lets them camp on our land. Sometimes he goes with them for weeks. He likes wild animals. He keeps a leopard and an ape as pets. The animals go all over the grounds whenever they want to. They frighten the people as much as he does.

"You can guess that Julia and I weren't very happy. No servant would stay with us. So we had to do all the housework ourselves. She was only thirty when she died. But her hair had already turned white, as mine is doing now."

"Your sister is dead, then?"

"She died just two years ago. That's one reason I've come to see you. You see, we had little chance to meet people and have friends. But we did visit our aunt sometimes. Julia was there at Christmas, two years ago. She met a soldier there and got engaged to him. My stepfather found out about it when she got home. He said nothing against her getting married at all. But two weeks before she was to be married this terrible thing happened."

Sherlock Holmes had been leaning back in his chair with his eyes closed. Now he half opened his eyes and looked at our visitor.

"Tell me everything about it," he said.

"That will be easy. I'll never forget any of it as long as I live. As I told you, the house is very old. We live in only one part of it. The bedrooms are on the ground floor. The first bedroom is Dr. Roylott's, the second was my sister's, and the third my own. There are no doors between them. All the bedroom doors open into the same hall, though. Is that clear?"

"Perfectly."

"The bedroom windows open out on the lawn. That night Dr. Roylott had gone to his room early. We knew he was not asleep, for my sister could smell the strong Indian cigars which he smoked. The smoke bothered my sister, so she came into my room. She stayed for a long time, talking about her coming wedding. At eleven o'clock she got up to leave. She stopped in the door and looked back.

" 'Tell me something, Helen,' she said. 'Have you heard anyone whistle during the night?'

" 'Never,' I said.

" 'I suppose you couldn't whistle, yourself, in your sleep?'

" 'I know I couldn't. But why?'

" 'Because during the last few nights I've heard a low clear whistle. It comes about three in the morning. I am a light sleeper, and it wakens me. I can't tell where it comes from. Perhaps it comes from the next room. Perhaps it comes from the lawn. I wondered if you had heard it.'

" 'No, I have not. It must be those gypsies.'

" 'I guess so. But if it came from the lawn you should have heard it, too.'

" 'Yes, but I'm harder to wake than you.'

" 'Well, it doesn't matter.' She smiled and closed the door. I heard her turn the key in the lock on her door."

"Did you always lock yourselves in at night?" asked Holmes.

"Always."

"Why?"

"I told you about the animals my stepfather keeps. We wouldn't feel safe unless we did."

"I see. Go on."

"I couldn't sleep that night. I felt that something was going to happen. It was a wild night. The wind was howling. The rain was beating against the windows. Suddenly above the storm came the scream of a woman. I knew it was my sister's voice. I sprang from my bed. Out into the hall I rushed. As I opened my door I heard a low whistle. Then I heard a clanging sound, as if a lot of metal had fallen. I ran down the hall. My sister's door was swinging open. By the light of the hall lamp I saw my sister come to the door. I could see she was terribly scared. She was reaching out with her hands. Her body swung back and forth, as if she were

8

drunk. I ran to her and threw my arms around her. But her knees gave way, and she fell to the floor. She twisted around as if she were in great pain. At first I thought she didn't know me. But as I bent over her she screamed, 'Helen, Helen! It was the band! The speckled band!' She wanted to say something else. She pointed her finger toward the doctor's room. Then she choked. I rushed out, calling for my stepfather. He came running from his room. He rushed to my sister's side. He poured brandy down her throat and sent for help. But she died without coming to. And that was the end of Julia."

"Just a minute," said Holmes. "Are you sure about the whistle and the clanging sound? Could you swear to it?"

"That's what they asked me in court. I'm sure I heard it, but the storm was loud. Maybe I was mistaken."

"Was your sister dressed?"

"She was in her nightgown. In her right hand was a burned match. In her left hand was a matchbox."

"That shows she had lit the match and looked around. That is important. What did the court decide?"

"They did everything they could. But they could

not tell why Julia had died. They knew that the door had been locked from the inside. The windows were blocked by shutters and iron bars. The walls were tested and found to be solid. The floor was the same. The chimney is wide, but is blocked by iron bars. My sister was surely alone. And she didn't have a mark on her."

"How about poison?"

"The doctors looked for poison but found none."

"What do you think killed her?"

"I think she died from fear. But I don't know what frightened her."

"Were the gypsies on your land then?"

"Yes. Some are nearly always there."

"What do you think she meant by the band—the speckled band?"

"Sometimes I think she was out of her head. Sometimes I think she meant a band of people—perhaps the gypsies. Some of them wear spotted handkerchiefs on their heads. Maybe that's what she meant."

Holmes shook his head. I knew he wasn't satisfied.

"Go on with your story," he said.

"That was two years ago. Until lately I've been more lonesome than ever. Just a month ago I became engaged. My stepfather has said nothing against my marriage. I am to be married in the spring. Two days ago some men came to do repairs on our house. I have had to move into the room which my sister had. I sleep in the same bed she slept in. Last night I heard that same clear whistle which came before she died. I sprang from my bed and lit the lamp. But I saw nothing. I was too much frightened to go back to sleep. I dressed, and as soon as it was daylight, I left to come to you."

"You have been wise," said Sherlock Holmes. "But have you told me everything?"

"Yes, everything."

"Miss Roylott, you have not. You are protecting your stepfather."

"Why, what do you mean?"

Holmes reached over and pushed back her sleeve. Five black and blue spots showed on her wrist. They were the marks of four fingers and a thumb.

"You have been hurt," said Holmes.

The lady turned her head and covered her wrist. "He is a hard man," she said. "He doesn't know how strong he is."

We were all quiet for a few minutes. Holmes looked into the fire.

"This is a deep business," he said at last. "There are many things I want to know before I do anything. We must move fast. Can we see those bedrooms today without your stepfather's knowing it?"

12

"He's in London today, on business. I think he will be gone all day. We have an old housekeeper now, but I can get her away."

"Good! Are you willing to go, Watson?"

"Willing and ready."

"Then Watson and I shall go. What are you going to do, Miss Roylott?"

"I have one or two things to do here in town. I'll go back on the twelve o'clock train and be waiting for you."

"We'll be there early in the afternoon. I have a few things to do myself. Will you wait and have some breakfast?"

"No, I must go. I feel much better since I've talked to you. I'll see you this afternoon." She dropped her black veil over her face and left.

"Well, Watson, what do you think of it?" asked Sherlock Holmes.

"It's a bad business, Holmes."

"Bad enough."

"Still, the floor and the walls were solid. No one could get through the door, the window, or the chimney. The sister must have been alone."

"But what about the whistle at night? And how about her dying words?"

"I can't explain that."

"Well, this is what we know. Someone did whistle

during the night. There were gypsies on the grounds. They were friends of the stepfather. The stepfather loses money if Helen marries. The dying sister said something about a band. Helen heard a clanging sound. Such a sound could be made by the iron bars on the windows."

"But what did the gypsies do?"

"That I can't tell you yet. I don't know that the gypsies did anything. That's why we're going out there today. I'm going to find out. Who—"

Holmes stopped. The door flew open. There stood a giant of a man. He was so tall that his hat touched the door frame. He seemed to fill the whole doorway. He had a large yellow face, full of wrinkles. His eyes were fierce and his large hooked nose made him look like a great eagle.

"Which one of you is Sherlock Holmes?" he growled.

"I am Sherlock Holmes," said my friend quietly. "And who are you?"

"I am Doctor Roylott."

"Well, Doctor," said Holmes smoothly, "won't you sit down?"

"I will not. My stepdaughter has been here. I followed her. What has she been telling you?"

"It's rather cold today, isn't it?" said Holmes.

"What did she tell you?" screamed Roylott.

14

"But perhaps it will be warmer soon," said Holmes.

"So you won't tell me?" yelled Roylott. He stepped forward and shook his fist. "I know you, you sneak! I have heard of you before. You're nosey Sherlock Holmes!"

Holmes smiled.

"Holmes, the busybody!"

Holmes' smile grew broader.

"Holmes, the stooge for Scotland Yard!"

Holmes threw back his head and laughed. "You're very funny," he said. "When you go, close the door, please."

"I'll go when I want to. You keep your nose out of my business. I know my stepdaughter was here. I followed her. And I'm a dangerous man to cross. See here." He stepped forward quickly and picked up our heavy poker. He bent it into a curve with his big brown hands.

"See that you stay out of my grip," he snarled. He fired the twisted poker into the fireplace, turned, and walked away.

"He seems to be a very friendly man," said Holmes, laughing. He picked up the steel poker and bent it straight again.

"Well, this makes the case more interesting. I hope the stepdaughter won't suffer for it. And now, Watson, let's get our breakfast. I have a few things

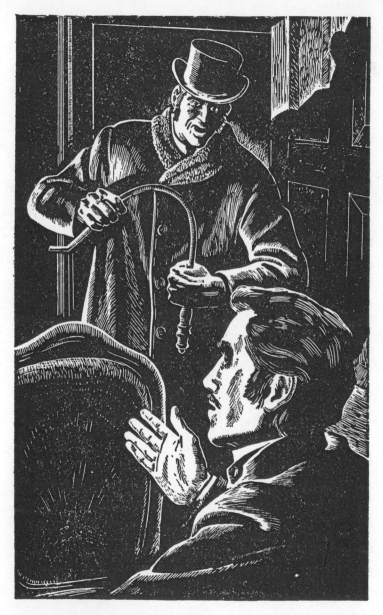

I want to check on before we leave this morning."

It was nearly one o'clock when Holmes got back. He had a sheet of paper filled with figures.

"I've looked up the will of the dead wife," he said. "And I've done a lot of figuring on what the stocks and bonds are bringing in today. When the wife died, they were bringing in almost 1100 pounds a year. Now they are worth about 750 pounds a year. Each daughter was to get 250 pounds a year out of that when she married. If they both married, he wouldn't have had much left. If only one married, it would cut him down. Well, I haven't wasted my time. He has a good reason not to want the girl to marry. And now, Watson, let's go. This is serious. And Roylott knows we're interested. If you're ready, call a cab. Slip your gun in your pocket. A gun is the best argument for a man who twists steel pokers. That and a toothbrush will be all we need."

We caught a train and were soon at the little country station. Here we got a man to drive us out to the Roylott home. Holmes sat in the front seat with his arms folded. His hat was pulled down over his eyes. Suddenly he looked up. He tapped me on the shoulder and pointed over the country fields.

"Look there!" he said.

I saw a hill thick with trees. Near the top I saw the gray roof of a big old house.

"Is that it?" asked Holmes.

"Yes, sir," said the driver. "That's Dr. Roylott's place."

"Oh, yes," said Holmes. "I see there is building going on. That's where we're going."

"There's the town over there." The driver pointed to the left. "If you want to get to the house, get off here. You can climb the wall and go up that path. It's shorter. There's the path where the lady is walking."

"And the lady is Miss Roylott," said Holmes. "Yes, we'll get off here."

We got off and paid the driver. Helen Roylott met us as we climbed the wall.

"Good afternoon, Miss Roylott," said Holmes. "Here we are, as we promised."

Helen Roylott was glad to see us. She shook hands warmly.

"I've been waiting for you. Everything is all right. Dr. Roylott is in town. I don't think he'll be back before evening."

"We met him," said Holmes. He quickly told her what had happened. Helen Roylott turned white.

"Oh!" she cried. "Then he followed me!"

"It looks like it."

"He is so cunning I never know when I'm safe from him. What will he say when he comes back?"

"He'd better be very careful. He's going to find us on his track. Lock yourself up tonight. If he is too angry, we'll take you to your aunt's. Now, we must hurry. Show us those bedrooms."

The house was built of gray stone. The middle part of the building was tallest. The side parts came out like two curving wings. In one of the wings the windows were broken and boarded up. The roof was partly caved in. The middle part didn't look much better. The second wing was fairly new. The blinds were on the windows, and smoke came from the chimney. Someone had been working on the building, but we saw no workers. Holmes walked slowly up and down the lawn. He examined the windows carefully.

"This, I guess, is the room where you used to sleep. This center one was your sister's. This one next to the main building is your stepfather's. Is that right?"

"That's right. But now I sleep in the middle room."

"Until the workers finish, I guess. I don't see just what they are fixing here."

"I don't think they are needed. I believe it's just an excuse to move me from my room."

"I see. Now the hall runs through this wing,

doesn't it? Are there windows anywhere in it?"

"Yes, but they are very small. No one could get through them."

"And you lock your door. No one could get in from that side. Now, go inside and close the shutters in your room."

Holmes tried as hard as he could to open the shutters from outside. He couldn't even slip a knife blade into a crack. Then he took out his magnifying lens and tested the hinges. They were of solid iron, built into the wall. "Nobody can get through this way," he said at last. "Let's see what the inside is like."

A small door opened into the hall outside the three bedrooms. We went right into the middle one which Helen Roylott was now using. It had a low ceiling and a big fireplace. A chest of drawers stood in one corner. In the other corner was a narrow bed. A dresser stood at the left of the window. Two wicker chairs and a small rug finished up the room. The woodwork was brown oak, hundreds of years old. Holmes pulled a chair into a corner and sat. He said nothing. His eyes moved slowly to every part of the room.

"What is that bell for?" he asked. He pointed to a thick bell-rope. It hung from the wall beside the bed. The tassel at the end lay on the pillow.

"It rings in the housekeeper's room."

"It looks fairly new."

"Yes, it's been there only a couple of years."

"Your sister asked for it?"

"No. She never used it. We got what we wanted ourselves."

"I don't know why anyone wants a bell-pull there. Well, I want to look at the floor. Excuse me." He threw himself on the floor. He crawled backward and forward with his lens. Very carefully he looked at each crack in the floor. Then he did the same with the woodwork. At last he walked over to the bed. He looked up and down the wall. Finally he took the bell-rope in his hand and pulled it.

"Why, it's a dummy," he said.

"Won't it ring?"

"No. It's not even on a wire. This is very interesting. See there! It's fastened to a hook. There, just above the little opening for the ventilator."

"Why, how strange! I never saw that before!" said Helen.

"Very strange!" said Holmes, pulling at the rope. "Now why would a builder run a ventilator into the next room? Why not to the outside?"

"That ventilator has been there only a few years," said Helen Roylott. "The builder didn't put it there."

"At the same time the bell-rope was put in?"

"Yes. Several little changes were made then."

"They are interesting changes. Dummy bell-ropes and ventilators which don't ventilate. Let's look at the other bedroom, Miss Roylott."

Dr. Roylott's bedroom was larger. In it he had a camp-bed. There were a small shelf of books, an armchair, a wooden chair, a round table, and a large iron safe. Holmes walked around slowly and looked at them all.

"What's in here?" he asked, tapping the safe.

"My stepfather's business papers."

"Have you ever looked inside?"

"Only once, years ago. I remember it was full of papers."

"There isn't a cat in it?"

"No. Why a cat?"

"Well, look at this!" He picked up a saucer of milk from the top of the safe.

"No, we don't keep a cat. But there are the other animals."

"Ah, yes. A leopard is just a big cat. Still, a saucer of milk would hardly feed it. Now, there's one thing I want to know." Holmes kneeled in front of the wooden chair. He examined the seat carefully.

"There. That's all right. Say, here is something interesting."

Holmes was looking at a small dog lead. It hung

from one corner of the bed. It had a loop tied in it.

"What do you think of this, Watson?"

"It's just a dog lead. I don't know why it should have a loop in it."

"That is strange, isn't it? Ah, me! This is a bad world, Watson. When a smart man turns to crime, it's worse. I think I've seen enough. Let's walk out on the lawn."

I had never seen Holmes look so serious. We walked up and down the lawn a few times. Neither Miss Roylott nor I said anything.

"Listen to me, Miss Roylott," he said. "This is important. You must do as I tell you."

"I will, Mr. Holmes."

"Your life depends on it."

"I will do just what you say."

"Watson and I must stay in your room tonight."

Miss Roylott and I looked at him in surprise.

"Yes, we must. Here's what we'll do. Is that building there in the distance the town hotel?"

"Yes."

"Good. Could we see your windows from there?"

"Oh, yes, easily."

"When your stepfather comes back, go to your room. Say you have a headache. Wait till he goes to bed. Then open the shutters of your window. Put your lamp in the window. Take what you need and go to your old room. You can stay there tonight, can't you?"

"Oh, yes."

"Leave the rest to us."

"But what will you do?"

"We'll spend the night in your room. We're going to find out about that whistle."

"I believe you know already, Mr. Holmes."

"Maybe I do."

"Then tell me how my sister died."

"I want to have the proof before I speak."

"Well, tell me this. Did she die from fright?"

"No, I don't think so. But, Miss Roylott, we must go. If Dr. Roylott should see us, everything would fail. Good-bye, and be brave. Do what I tell you. You will soon be out of danger."

Sherlock Holmes and I got rooms in the little hotel in town. They were on the top floor. From the windows we could see the Roylott house easily. Just as it was getting dark we saw Dr. Roylott pass on the road. A few minutes later a light went on in one of the rooms.

"Watson," said Holmes, "I don't know whether you should come along tonight. There's great danger."

"Would I be of any help to you?"

"Yes, I think you would."

"Then I'm coming with you, of course."

"Thank you."

"You talk of danger. You must have seen something I didn't see."

"No, you saw everything I saw. Some things may have meant more to me, though."

"I saw nothing strange except the bell-rope. And I don't know what that could have to do with the case."

"You saw the ventilator?"

"Yes, but what was so strange about that? It was so small a rat could hardly get through it."

"I knew we'd find a ventilator before we got to the house."

"Oh, come, now, Holmes. Not really?"

"Oh, yes, I did. You remember she said her sister could smell the cigar. I knew there must be an opening between the two rooms. It had to be a small one or the police would have seen it when the sister died. I thought it must be a ventilator."

"But what harm is the ventilator?"

"Well, think about this. A ventilator is made. A bell-rope is hung. A woman who sleeps in the bed dies. How about that?"

"I don't see any connection."

"Did you see anything strange about the bed?"

"No."

"It was clamped to the floor. Did you ever see that before?"

"No, I haven't."

"She couldn't move her bed. It had to stay near the ventilator. It had to stay near the rope."

"Holmes!" I cried. "I begin to see what you are driving at. We are just in time to stop a horrible crime."

"Yes, it's horrible. When a doctor goes wrong, he is the worst of criminals. He has nerve and he knows things. This man is clever. We shall have to be more clever. But it's going to be bad enough tonight. Let's smoke a pipe and think of other things for a few hours."

Roylott's light went out about nine o'clock. Everything was dark at the house. Two hours passed slowly by. Suddenly as the clock struck eleven, a bright light shone out.

"That's our signal," said Holmes, jumping to his feet. "It's from the middle window."

As we left, Holmes spoke to the man at the hotel desk. He told him we were going on a late visit to a friend and that we might stay for the night. A minute later we were out on the dark road. A cold wind blew in our faces. We headed for the light from the house.

We climbed the old stone wall and made our way

26

through the trees. We reached the lawn and crossed it. Just as we were getting ready to climb through the window, we heard a sound. From behind some bushes jumped what looked like a horrible child. It threw itself twisting on the grass. Then it leaped up and ran into the darkness.

"Holmes!" I whispered. "Did you see it?"

His hand closed like iron on my wrist. But then he gave a low laugh. "The ape," he whispered.

I had forgotten the doctor's strange pets. There was a leopard, too. I thought of it landing with a snarl on our shoulders. I felt a lot better a minute later. We took off our shoes and climbed into the bedroom. Holmes closed the shutters softly. He moved the lamp to the table and looked around the room. Everything was the same. He put his mouth to my ear and whispered:

"Don't dare make a sound."

I nodded my head to show I'd heard.

"Can't have a light. He'd see it through the ventilator."

I nodded again.

"Don't go to sleep. Your life depends on it. Have your gun ready. I'll sit on the bed. You can sit on that chair."

I took out my gun and laid it on the table. Holmes had brought a long thin cane. He laid it on the

27

bed. He now laid a box of matches and a candle next to it. Then he turned out the light.

I'll never forget that night. I couldn't hear a sound in the room. The shutters kept out all light. Sometimes a bird would call outside. Once we heard a long cat-like cry. I remembered the leopard and shivered. The clock down in the town struck the hours. Twelve. Then one, then two, finally three!

Suddenly a gleam of light came from the ventilator. Darkness again. Then a smell of burning oil and hot metal. Someone in the next room had lit a lantern. A little sound—then quiet again. The smell grew stronger. For another half hour we sat.

Then suddenly I heard another sound. It was a soft, whispering sound—like steam coming from a kettle. The instant we heard it Holmes leaped from the bed. He struck a match and whipped his cane at the bell-rope.

"You see it, Watson?" he yelled. "You see it?"

But I saw nothing. When Holmes lit the match I heard a low clear whistle. I couldn't see what he was swinging at. His face was white and his eyes flashed.

He had stopped hitting at the rope. Now he stood looking at the ventilator. Suddenly a horrible scream burst out. It grew louder and louder. We heard later that it woke people in town. My heart felt cold inside me and I shook with a chill. I looked at Holmes and he looked at me.

"What does it mean?"

"It's all over," Holmes said. "I guess it's best this way. Take your gun. We're going into Dr. Roylott's room."

He lit the lamp and we went into the hall. He knocked twice at the door. There was no answer. He turned the handle and went in. I followed, gun in my hand.

It was a strange sight we saw. On the table stood a lamp. The light shone on the open door of the safe. Beside the table, on the wooden chair, sat Dr. Roylott. He was dressed in a long gray robe. His bare feet rested on the heels. His chin was pushed forward. His eyes were wide open, staring at the ceiling. Tight around his head was a yellow band with brown speckles. He didn't move.

"The band! The speckled band!" whispered Holmes.

I stepped forward. The strange head band began to move. Out of his hair there rose the diamond-shaped head of a horrible snake!

"It's a swamp adder, a swamp snake," cried Holmes. "It's the most deadly snake in India. He died in ten seconds after it bit him. Let's get it where it belongs and get Helen Roylott out of here."

He picked the dog lead out of Roylott's lap. Then he slipped the loop over the snake's head and pulled it tight. Holding it from him, he carried it to the safe. He threw it inside and slammed the door.

And that's the adventure of the speckled band. We told Helen Roylott the whole story and sent her on to her aunt's home. The police were called in. They decided Dr. Roylott had been bitten while playing with his pet snake. The next day Holmes and I were on our way back to London.

"I was off the track at first, Watson," he said. "The girl had used the word 'band.' And there was a band of gypsies on the place. But I soon saw no one could get in through the window or the door. Then I saw the ventilator and the bell-rope. The bell-rope was a dummy. The bed was clamped to the floor. I thought of a snake right away. The doctor had other strange pets. Why not a snake? No one would think of snake poison when the girl died. And who would see the two tiny holes of the snake's bite? Then I thought of the whistle. The doctor had to get the snake back. So he trained it. He gave it milk whenever it came at his whistle. He'd put the snake in the ventilator. He knew it would crawl down the rope and land on the bed. Maybe it would bite, maybe it wouldn't. But sooner or later it would.

"I had all this figured out before I looked at his room. I looked carefully at his chair. He'd been standing on it, for he'd scratched it. I knew he used it to reach the ventilator. Then I saw the safe, the milk, and the dog lead. That made it sure. The clanging sound Helen had heard was the slamming of the safe door. When I heard the snake hiss, I went after it with my cane."

"To drive it back through the ventilator?"

"Yes, and to go after Dr. Roylott. When I hit it, the snake got angry. It went for the first person it saw. So, I guess, I am the cause of Dr. Roylott's death. But, Watson, I'm not going to lose any sleep over *that*."

The Red-Headed League

ONE day last autumn I called on my friend Mr. Sherlock Holmes. I found him talking with a fat man with red hair.

"Pardon me, Holmes," I said. "I didn't know—"

But Holmes quickly pulled me into the room and closed the door.

"My dear Watson," said Holmes, "I'm glad you came."

"I was afraid you were busy."

"I am. Very busy."

"Then I can wait in the next room."

"Not at all." Holmes turned to the red-headed man.

"This gentleman, Mr. Wilson, is my partner. He has been with me in most of my best cases. I know he will help me with yours."

The fat man looked me over carefully.

"Sit down, Watson," said Holmes. "I know you like these strange cases. You have written enough about them."

"Yes," I said, "I am interested in your cases. Very much interested."

"Now, Mr. Wilson here came to see me this morning. He's started to tell me his story. I think it's going to be a good one. Mr. Wilson, will you start from the beginning again? I'd like to hear every bit once more. I don't think I've ever heard one like it."

The fat Mr. Wilson pulled a dirty newspaper from his overcoat. He put the paper on his knee and turned to the ads. I looked at him very carefully, as Holmes had taught me to do.

I didn't see anything unusual about him. He was just a business man of some kind. He wore a pair of gray trousers and a black coat. A thick watch chain hung from his vest pocket. I noticed a square piece of metal on the chain. A worn black hat and a wrinkled brown overcoat lay on a chair. I looked and looked again, but I could see nothing unusual. Nothing except that he had bright red hair and was angry about something.

Sherlock Holmes smiled when he saw what I was doing.

"Oh," he said, "you can't tell much about him,

Watson. He has done some hard work in his life. He takes snuff. He belongs to the Masons. He's been in China. He's done a lot of writing lately. That's about all."

Wilson jumped out of his chair. "How did you know all that, Mr. Holmes?" he asked. "How did you know I've done hard work? It's true. I was a ship's carpenter once."

"Your hands, Mr. Wilson. Your right hand is a little bigger than the left one. You've worked with it. The muscles are bigger."

"Well, the Masons, then?"

Holmes pointed to the pin on his coat.

"Oh, yes. I forgot that. But the writing? How did you know that?"

"Look at that right cuff. Five inches of it is shiny. And there's a shiny spot near the left elbow. That's where you lay it on the desk."

"How did you know I've been in China?"

"By that fish you have tattooed on your right wrist. It can be done only in China. I've made a study of tattoo marks. Only the Chinese can get that pink color on the fish scales. Also, you have a Chinese coin on your watch chain."

Wilson laughed. "Well, well," he said. "I thought you'd done something very clever. I see it was easy, after all."

"You see, Watson," said Holmes, "I shouldn't explain these things. It looks so easy when I do. But go on, Wilson. Have you found the ad?"

"Yes, I have it. Here it is. This started it all. You go ahead and read it."

I took the paper. This is what I read.

There is now another job open in the Red-Headed League. This League was started with the money left by Mr. E. Hopkins of Pennsylvania, U. S. A. The pay is four pounds a week for little work. Any red-headed men over twenty-one may try out. Ask for Duncan Ross, at the offices of the Red-Headed League, 7 Pope's Court, Fleet Street. Come in person on Monday, at eleven o'clock.

"What on earth does this mean?" I said.

Holmes smiled. "It is a strange one, isn't it? And now, Mr. Wilson. Tell us all about it. What paper is that, Watson? And what date?"

"The London *Times* of July 27, 1890. Two months ago."

"Good. Go on, Mr. Wilson."

"Well, it's just as I've been telling you, Mr. Sherlock Holmes. I have a little pawnbroker's business in the city. I lend money to people on jewels and clothing and other things. When they don't come back, I make something by selling them. It's not a big place. Lately I've made a living and that's about all. I used to keep two clerks. Now I have only one. I wouldn't be able to pay him, but he works for half pay. He wants to learn the business."

"Who is this kind-hearted fellow?" asked Holmes.

"His name is Vincent Spaulding. I don't know just how old he is. I wouldn't want a smarter clerk. He could make twice as much somewhere else. But if he wants to work for me, why should I worry?"

"You're lucky to have a good clerk for half pay," said Holmes. "Workers are hard to get these days. I'm surprised that you can keep him."

"Oh, he has his faults, too," said Mr. Wilson. "I never saw such a fellow for taking pictures. He's always running down to the cellar to develop them. That's all that's wrong with him, though. He's a good worker."

"He's still working for you?"

"Yes, sir. He and a girl who cooks and keeps the place clean. I'm not married and have no family."

"Go on."

"Well, just eight weeks ago we saw this ad. Spaulding came in with this very paper in his hand. He says,

" 'I wish I were a red-headed man, Mr. Wilson.'

" 'Why?' I asks.

" 'Why,' says he, 'here's another job open in the League of Red-Headed Men. They tell me you have hardly anything to do and you get good pay. If my

37

hair could only change its color, I'd have that job.'

" 'What kind of job is it?' I asks. You see, Mr. Holmes, I don't know much of what goes on. I don't read the newspapers and I usually stay at home.

" 'Haven't you heard of the League of the Red-Headed Men?' he asks, sort of surprised.

" 'Never.'

" 'That's funny. I thought all you red-headed fellows knew about it.'

" 'What does the job pay?' I asks.

" 'Oh, just a couple of hundred pounds a year. But the work is easy. You can do it part time.'

"Well, you can guess I got interested. The business wasn't very good. A couple of hundred pounds would come in handy.

" 'Tell me all about it,' said I.

" 'Well,' he said, 'you can see for yourself. The League has a job open. You go here to ask for it. Here's the way I get it. This Hopkins started the League. He was an American millionaire. He had red hair, and he liked everybody else who had red hair. When he died, he left all his money for red-headed men. Easy jobs for redheads.'

" 'But,' I said, 'won't there be millions of red-headed men after the jobs?'

" 'Not so many,' he answered. 'You have to live in London. You have to be a grown man. This

Hopkins got his start here in London. He wants to do something for the old town. And you don't get in if you have light or dark red hair. You must have bright, fiery red hair. Why, Mr. Wilson, if you wanted the job, I'll bet you could get it. But I guess you don't need the money.'

"Now, Mr. Holmes, you see I do have bright red hair. I thought I'd have a good chance at the job. Vincent Spaulding knew a lot about it, so I took him along. We started out for the place.

"I'll never see so many red-headed men again. They came from north, south, east, and west. Everybody with any red in his hair was there to answer that ad. When I saw them all, I wanted to go back home. But Vincent Spaulding wouldn't listen to it. I don't know how he did it. He pushed and pulled and butted. At last he got me through the crowd. Some were coming out. We kept pushing. Then we got into the office."

"Very interesting," said Sherlock Holmes. "What happened then?"

"There was nothing in the office but a couple of chairs and a table. There sat a small man with hair even redder than mine. He'd say a few words to each man. But he always had some reason for not taking him. When my turn came he closed the door.

" 'This is Mr. Wilson,' said Vincent Spaulding.

39

'He's come for that job for a man with red hair.'

" 'And he just may get it, too,' answered the man. 'He really has the right color. I don't know when I've seen one this good.' He took a step backward. He turned his head to one side, looking at me carefully. Then he grabbed my hand and shook it.

" 'You're the man,' he said. 'Please pardon me.' He quickly reached out, grabbed my hair, and pulled. I yelled with pain.

" 'Ah!' he said, 'there's water in your eyes. Everything is all right. We have to be careful, you see. Two men already have fooled us with wigs.' He stepped to the window and shouted that the job was filled.

" 'My name is Duncan Ross,' he said. 'When shall you be ready to start work?'

" 'Well,' I answered, 'I don't know. I have my own business.'

" 'Oh, never mind about that, Mr. Wilson!' said Vincent Spaulding. 'I'll be able to look after that for you.'

" 'What would be the hours?' I asked.

" 'Ten until two.'

"Now a pawnbroker does most of his work at night, Mr. Holmes. Thursday and Friday are heavy days. That's just before pay day. I was glad to work at those hours. I knew that Vincent Spaulding was

40

a good man. He could take care of things for me.

" 'That suits me fine,' I said. 'How about the pay?'

" 'It's four pounds a week.'

" 'And the work?'

" 'Nothing to it.'

" 'What do you mean by that?'

" 'Well, you have to be in this office. At least you can't leave the building. If you do, you lose the job.'

" 'It's only four hours a day. I won't leave,' said I.

" 'No excuses will do,' said Mr. Duncan Ross. 'Not even if you're sick. Stay or lose the job.'

" 'What's the work?'

" 'You copy the Encyclopedia Britannica. There is the first book. You bring ink, pens, and paper. Will you be ready tomorrow?'

" 'Yes,' I said.

" 'Then, good-bye, Mr. Wilson. I'm glad you have the job.'

"I went home with Vincent Spaulding. I didn't know what to say, I was so glad about my good luck.

"Well, I thought about it all day. By evening I was feeling pretty low. I was sure somebody was playing a joke on me. Who on earth would make such a silly will? And who would pay people to copy an encyclopedia? Vincent Spaulding did his best to cheer me up. In the morning I thought I'd

42

try it, anyway. I bought paper, ink, and a pen and started out.

"Well, everything was all right, after all. The table was ready. Duncan Ross was there to get me started. He started me with the letter A and then left me. Once in a while he'd come in to see me. At two o'clock he came back again. He said I had done very well. He said good-bye and locked the door after me.

"This went on day by day, Mr. Holmes. On Saturday Mr. Ross came in and paid me my four pounds. It was the same the next week. And the week after that. Every morning I came at ten. Every afternoon I left at two. Mr. Ross now came in only once in the morning. After a while he stopped coming. But I didn't dare leave. The job was too good.

"Eight weeks went by. I wrote and wrote. I was almost finished with the A's. Then it was all over."

"All over?"

"Yes, sir. This morning I went to work as usual. But the door was locked. Someone had nailed a card on the door. Here it is. Read it yourself."

He held up a white card. This is what it said:

The Red-Headed League

is no more

October 9, 1890

Wilson looked so sad that Holmes and I had to laugh. "I can't see anything funny," cried Wilson. "If you want to laugh about it, I can go somewhere else."

"No, no," cried Holmes. He jumped up and pushed Wilson back into his chair. "I wouldn't miss this case for anything. But it is a little funny. What did you do when you saw the card?"

"I didn't know what to do. I asked at some of the other offices. No one knew anything about the Red-Headed League. At last I went to the landlord and asked about the League. He said he'd never heard of it. Then I asked him who Duncan Ross was. He said he'd never heard of him.

" 'Well,' I said, 'the man in No. 4.'

" 'What, the red-headed man?'

" 'Yes.'

" 'Oh,' he said, 'his name was William Morris. He was a lawyer. He moved out yesterday.'

" 'Where can I find him?'

" 'At his new offices. He did tell me the address. Yes, 17 King Edward Street.'

"I started off, Mr. Holmes. But when I arrived, I found it was a factory. No one there had ever heard of Mr. William Morris or Mr. Duncan Ross."

"And what did you do then?" asked Holmes.

"I went home and talked it over with Vincent

Spaulding. But he couldn't help me. He said to wait. He thinks I'll hear from Mr. Ross by mail. I heard that you help people, so I came right away to you."

"You did right," said Holmes. "Your case is very unusual. I'll be glad to see about it. I think it is more serious than you think."

"It's serious enough!" said Wilson. "Why, I've lost four pounds a week."

"I don't see that you have any kick coming," said Holmes. "You made about thirty pounds. You even learned a lot. No, you haven't lost anything."

"No, sir. But I want to find out about them. Who is this man Duncan Ross? Why did he play this joke on me? It cost him thirty-two pounds."

"We'll try to find out for you. Now I want to ask you a question or two. This fellow Spaulding. How long had he been working for you when he showed you the ad?"

"About a month."

"How did you get him?"

"He answered an ad I put in the paper."

"Was he the only one who answered the ad?"

"No, there were ten or twelve."

"Why did you pick him?"

"Because he was smart and would work cheap."

"At half pay?"

"Yes, he said he was willing to do that."

"What's he like?"

"He's small and very quick. He's about thirty years old, I guess. Has a white scar on his forehead."

Holmes jumped up. "I thought so," he said. "Has he holes in his ears for earrings?"

"Yes, sir. He told me a gypsy had done it for him when he was a boy."

"Hmm!" said Holmes. "Is he still with you?"

"Oh, yes, sir. I just left him."

"Did he take care of your business pretty well?"

"I guess so. There's not much to do during the day."

"That will be all, Mr. Wilson. Today is Saturday. By Monday I'll be able to tell you something."

"Well, Watson," said Sherlock Holmes when Wilson was gone. "What do you think?"

"I don't know, Holmes. It's a mystery to me."

"The mysterious cases are usually the simple ones. The cases that look simple are often hard ones. I'll have to get busy."

"What are you going to do?"

"I'm going to smoke. Don't talk to me for about an hour."

He curled up in his chair and lit his pipe. He pulled his thin knees up to his hawk-like nose. There he sat with his eyes closed. I thought he had gone to sleep. But after an hour he suddenly jumped up.

"Come on, Watson. There is a great violinist in town. He's playing this afternoon. You doctors can get away once in a while, can't you?"

"I guess I can."

"Then put on your hat. I have something else to do first. We can get our lunch on the way."

After we got to the city we walked past Wilson's place. It was a dirty, two-story brick house. A sign hung outside with his name on it. Sherlock Holmes stopped in front of the house. He looked it over very carefully. Then he walked slowly up the street. Back he came to the corner, looking keenly at all the houses. Finally he came back to Wilson's place. He pounded on the sidewalk two or three times with his stick. Then he suddenly went up to the door and knocked. A bright-looking young man opened the door.

"Come right in," he said.

"Thank you," said Holmes. "I just want some help. Where is the Crown Theatre, please?"

"Three blocks left and then four right." The door closed.

"Smart fellow," said Holmes. "He is the fourth smartest man in London. I know only two men more daring. I've had something to do with him before."

"You asked directions just to see him, didn't you?"

"Not him."

"What then?"

"The knees of his trousers."

"And what did you see?"

"What I thought I'd see."

"Why did you pound the sidewalk?"

"My dear doctor, this is no time for talk. Let's look around a little more."

We turned the corner and found ourselves on a big busy street.

"Let me see," said Holmes. "I want to remember what buildings are here. First comes the tobacco shop. Next, the newspaper office. There is the City Bank. Next comes a restaurant. Now Doctor, we've done our work. Let's get a sandwich and a cup of coffee. Then we go to hear that violin."

Sherlock Holmes loved music. He played the violin very well himself. He had even written some music. All afternoon he sat listening and was perfectly happy. He didn't look at all like the keen, sharp detective. But I had seen him change before. Usually it was after a time like this that he really turned loose on the law breakers. Now he was quiet and dreamy. Someone was going to have a bad time of it soon, I knew.

"You want to go home, I guess," he said as we

came out into the street after the concert.

"I suppose so," I answered.

"I have some work to do. This case of Wilson's is serious."

"Why serious?"

"A big crime has been planned. I think we'll be in time to stop it. But today is already Saturday. I'll need your help tonight."

"At what time?"

"Ten will be early enough."

"I'll be at your rooms in Baker Street by ten."

"Good. There may be some danger. Better put your army gun in your pocket." He waved his hand and walked off.

I think I'm about as smart as the next fellow. But every time I was in a case with Sherlock Holmes I felt stupid. Here I had heard what he had heard. I had seen what he had seen. He knew what had happened. He even knew what was going to happen. I didn't. As I went home I went over the whole story. Where were we going that night? Why should I carry a gun? Holmes had let me know that Spaulding was a dangerous man. I tried to puzzle it out. But I had to give up.

A little after nine I started for Baker Street. I went into the house and heard voices from Holmes' rooms. I found him talking with two men. One I knew. He was Peter Jones, a police detective. The other was a long, thin, sad-faced man. He had a shiny black hat and wore very good clothes.

"Ha! We are all here," said Holmes. He put on his coat. "Watson, you know Mr. Jones of Scotland Yard, don't you? I want you to meet Mr. Merryweather. Mr. Merryweather will go with us tonight."

"I hope it won't be a wild goose chase," said Mr. Merryweather.

"You can trust Mr. Holmes, sir," said the police detective. "He does things his own way. I don't think it's always the best way, but he may be a detective yet. I admit that he has been closer to the truth several times than we have."

"Oh, if you say so, Mr. Jones, it's all right," said Merryweather. "I hate to miss my game of cards tonight. I've played cards every Saturday night for twenty-seven years."

"You'll play for more tonight than you ever have," said Holmes. "And the game will be more exciting. You will be gambling for about 30,000 pounds, Merryweather. Jones, you will get a chance to catch a man you want badly."

"You're right, Holmes," said Jones. "John Clay is a killer and a thief and a few other things. I'd rather catch him than any other crook in London. He's quite a man, this John Clay. Had a rich family.

He's been to the best schools in England. His brain is as clever as his fingers. He'll crack a safe here one week and tap somebody on the head somewhere else the next week. I've been after him for years. And I've never even set eyes on him yet."

"I'm going to have you meet him tonight, Jones. I've had something to do with John Clay once or twice myself. He's a good one, all right. But it's past ten o'clock. We'd better start. You two go ahead. Watson and I will follow."

Sherlock Holmes said very little on the way. He lay back and hummed the tunes he'd heard that afternoon. When we got near Wilson's place he said:

"This fellow Merryweather is a big man in the City Bank. I thought Jones should come, too. He's not a bad fellow. Just stupid. He isn't bright, but he's brave as a bulldog. Here we are. They're waiting for us."

We were now on the same busy street we'd seen that morning. Merryweather led us to the bank. We went past the side of the building and up to a side door. Merryweather took out his keys and unlocked it. Inside was a hall which ended at a big iron gate. He unlocked this gate also. Now we went down the stone stairs. At the bottom we came to another iron gate. Merryweather stopped and lit a lantern. We next went through a small dark

52

passage. The next door was opened. Here we found ourselves in a big vault, or cellar. Big boxes were piled all around us to the ceiling.

"It would be pretty hard to get in here from above," said Holmes as he looked around.

"And from below," said Merryweather. He tapped his stick on the stone floor. "Why," he said, very much surprised, "it sounds hollow."

"You will have to be more quiet!" said Holmes angrily. "You have almost spoiled my little plan. You sit on one of those boxes. And don't move."

Merryweather looked as if he'd been spanked. He climbed on one of the boxes and didn't say a word. Holmes dropped on his knees. He pulled out his magnifying glass and looked at the floor carefully. He seemed to find what he wanted. He jumped up and put the glass in his pocket.

"We have at least an hour to wait," he said. "They won't move until Wilson's in bed. Then they'll move fast. The sooner they get their work done, the longer to make their get-away. You know we are in the cellar of the City Bank, Doctor. Mr. Merryweather will tell you why London crooks are interested in this cellar."

"It is our French gold," whispered Merryweather. "We were afraid someone would try to get it."

"Your French gold?"

"Yes. A few months ago we borrowed about 30,000 pounds of it from the Bank of France. Someone knows we haven't even unpacked it. This box I'm sitting on has 2,000 gold pounds in it."

"Well, let's get ready," said Holmes. "I think they'll be here in about an hour. Put a cover on that lantern."

"And sit in the dark?"

"Yes. First, get in the right places. These men are daring. If we're not careful, we may get hurt. I'll stand behind this box. You fellows hide over there. When I turn a light on them, jump on them. If they have guns, Watson, shoot them down."

I laid my gun on top of a box and got behind it. Holmes covered the lantern. Now it was pitch dark. I could smell the lantern and knew it was ready.

"They have only one way out," whispered Holmes. "That is back through Wilson's place. Did you do what I told you, Jones?"

"A detective and two policemen are at the front door."

"Good. We've stopped all the holes. Now, be quiet and wait."

It seemed to me we waited a year. I found out later it was about an hour. My legs got stiff and tired. But I didn't dare move. I could look over my box to the floor. Suddenly I saw a spark of light.

The spark grew longer and became a yellow line. Then the floor seemed to open. I saw a white hand in the light. It was pulled back quickly, and the light was gone. I still didn't hear a sound.

Then, with a sharp, tearing sound, one of the big white stones turned over. The light from a lantern poured out of the hole where the stone had lain. A head popped out and looked around quickly. The man put his hands on the sides of the hole and pulled himself up. He jumped to his feet and reached down to help another man up. The second man was small and had bright red hair.

"All clear," he whispered. "Got the bags? Great Scott! Jump, Archie, jump!"

Sherlock Holmes had thrown himself on the first one and had him on the floor. The other dived down the hole. I heard the cloth tear and saw Jones with a piece of his coat in his hands. The light flashed on a gun, but Holmes smashed the man's hand with his fist. The gun fell to the floor.

"It's no use, John Clay," said Holmes calmly. "You haven't a chance."

"I guess you're right," the other answered, as cool as could be. "But my pal is all right."

"There are three men waiting for him at the door," said Holmes.

"You have done well. I must compliment you."

"And I must compliment you," answered Holmes. "Your red-headed idea was a new one. And very clever."

"You'll see your pal right away," said Jones. "He's quicker at diving down holes than I am. Hold out your hands."

"Don't touch me with your dirty hands," said Clay as Jones put handcuffs on him. "And when you talk to me say 'sir' and 'please'."

Jones looked at him and started to laugh. "Well, would you please, sir, march upstairs? We'd like to take your Highness to jail."

"That's better," said John Clay. He bowed to the three of us and went with Jones.

"I don't know how the bank can thank you, Mr. Holmes," said Merryweather as we went up the stairs. "You have caught the cleverest bank robbers in London. How can we pay you?"

"Oh," said Holmes, "I just wanted to get John Clay. I've had a little expense. The bank can pay that back. I don't want anything more. I've had a fine time."

An hour later Holmes and I were in his rooms in Baker Street.

"You see, Watson," he explained, "it was easy. There was only one reason for the Red-Headed League. That was to get Wilson out of the way for a few hours a day. It was a strange way to do it, of course. Clay must have got the idea from his pal's red hair. But can you think of a better one? The four pounds a week was cheap. They were playing for thousands. So they put the ad in the paper. One crook stays in the office. The other one gets Wilson to answer the ad. And so they get him out of the house. When I heard Wilson's helper was working for half pay, I smelled a rat. There had to be a reason."

"But how did you guess the reason?"

"There was nothing in the house they wanted. So it had to be outside the house. What could it be? I thought of Spaulding always running down to the cellar. The cellar! That was it! So I asked about this Spaulding. I found he was John Clay, one of the coolest, most daring of the crooks in London. He was doing something in the cellar. He was doing something which took hours every day, for months. What could it be? The only thing I could think of was—a tunnel. He must be digging a tunnel to another building."

"Then we went to Wilson's place. I pounded the sidewalk with my stick. I was trying to find which way the tunnel ran. It was not in front. Then I rang the bell. Clay and I had never seen each other before, so there was no danger. I hardly looked at his face. I wanted to see his knees. Didn't you see how dirty they were? They showed he'd been digging.

"Now I needed to find out where they were going. I walked around the corner. There was the City Bank! I knew that was the answer. When you drove home I called Scotland Yard. Then I went to see Merryweather. The rest you know."

"How could you tell they would break in tonight?"

"When they broke up the Red-Headed League they were through with Wilson. That meant the tunnel was finished. They had to use it as soon as they could. The gold might be taken away any day. Saturday was best. The bank wouldn't open again until Monday. That gave them time to get far away. So I looked for them tonight."

"You figured it out beautifully," I cried.

"Oh, it kept me from being bored," he answered, yawning. "The little problems help me. I hope we get another good one soon."

The Adventure of the Six Napoleons

DETECTIVE Lestrade of Scotland Yard often came to see us at Baker Street. Sherlock Holmes liked to have him come. Lestrade kept him up to date on the police news. Holmes often helped him. Lestrade would tell him about his new cases. Then Holmes would give him some ideas to go ahead.

This evening Lestrade talked about the weather. Then he talked about the newspapers. And then he just sat, puffing his cigar. Holmes looked at him keenly.

"Anything new, Lestrade?" he asked.

"Oh, no, Mr. Holmes. Nothing big."

"Then tell me about it."

Lestrade laughed.

"Well, Mr. Holmes, I do have something on my mind. But it's so silly! I wasn't going to talk about it. It's funny. And you do like these strange cases. I think it's a case for Dr. Watson, though."

"Sickness?" I asked.

"No, someone must be crazy. Could anyone still hate Napoleon? Enough to go around breaking statues of him?"

Holmes sat back in his chair.

"That's no work for me," he said.

"That's what I say. But the man is breaking into houses. He breaks in and smashes these busts of Napoleon. They don't belong to him, so it's a police case."

"Ah, that's different! Let me hear about it."

Lestrade took out his notebook. He turned the pages.

"The first case came four days ago," he said. "It was at the shop of Morse Hudson. Mr. Hudson sells pictures and statues on Kennington Road. His man stepped out for a minute. Suddenly he heard a crash. He ran back in. There he found a plaster bust of Napoleon broken into a thousand pieces. He rushed out into the street. Some people told him a man had run out. He could see no one, though. He told the policeman on the beat about it. The plaster bust was not worth much, anyway. We didn't do anything more about it.

"Then came the second case. That happened last

night. A Dr. Barnicot lives near the Hudson shop, also on Kennington Road. He has an office on Brixton Road. Dr. Barnicot is interested in Napoleon. He has many pictures of him. He is always buying books about him. Not long ago he bought two busts of Napoleon from Hudson. He put one in his house on Kennington Road. He put the other in his office on the Brixton Road. Well, when Dr. Barnicot came down stairs this morning, he got a surprise. Someone had broken into his house. But only one thing was gone—his bust of Napoleon. Someone had taken it out into the yard. There he had smashed it against the garden wall. The pieces were still lying there."

Holmes rubbed his hands.

"This is very interesting," he said.

"I thought you'd like it. But I haven't finished. Dr. Barnicot went to his office at noon. There he got his second surprise. Someone had broken the window during the night. The broken pieces of the second bust were thrown around the room. It had been smashed, also. There were no clues. Now, Mr. Holmes, that's all we know."

"I've never run into anything just like this," said Holmes. "Were Dr. Barnicot's Napoleons just like Morse Hudson's?"

"They came from the same mold."

"Then the man doesn't hate Napoleon. There must be hundreds of Napoleon's statues in London. Why wouldn't he break others? Why take three from the same mold?"

"I thought that way, too," said Lestrade. "But look here. Hudson sells statues in that part of London. He has no other Napoleons. If this fellow lived there, that's where he'd start. What do you think, Dr. Watson?"

"Well, the man could be crazy. He could be crazy on Napoleon. He might have read a lot about him. One of his family could have been killed in a war."

"No, Watson," said Holmes, shaking his head. "That won't do."

"Well, how do you explain it?"

"I don't try to yet. But this fellow isn't crazy. Did you think of this? He takes the bust from Dr. Barnicot's home. He takes it outside to break it. Why? Because he would wake someone if he didn't. But at Barnicot's office he breaks it inside. Why? Because it's safer inside. No, he isn't crazy, Watson. This is an interesting case, Lestrade. Let me know what happens next, will you?"

Holmes found out what happened next in a hurry. The next morning I was dressing in my bedroom. I heard a tap on the door. Holmes came in. He had a telegram in his hand. He read it to me. It was signed by Lestrade. The message read: "Come quickly, 131 Pitt Street."

"What is it?" I asked.

"Don't know. May be anything. Something about the Napoleons. He's in another part of the city now. There's coffee on the table, Watson. I have a cab at the door."

In half an hour we reached Pitt Street. The street was a very quiet one. But there was a crowd in front of No. 131. Holmes whistled.

"By George! It looks like murder. What's this, Watson? The top steps washed off, the bottom ones dry. Well, well, there's Lestrade at the front window. We'll soon know about it."

Lestrade didn't even smile at us. He led us into the living room. Here a man was walking up and down.

"This is Mr. Harker, gentlemen. Mr. Holmes, it's the Napoleon bust thing again. You were interested last night. I thought you'd want to come."

"What's wrong?"

"Murder, Mr. Holmes. Mr. Harker here will tell you what happened."

Holmes sat down to listen.

"About four months ago I bought that bust of Napoleon. I picked it up cheap from Harding Brothers' store. I bought it for this very room. I work in here at night, doing a lot of writing. I went to bed late last night. My bedroom is upstairs. I thought I heard a noise down here. I listened, but heard nothing more. Then about five minutes later I heard a yell. I'll never forget it. I grabbed a poker. I came down the stairs. That window there was wide open. I saw that the bust was gone. I don't know why anybody would want it.

"You can see that a man can jump from the doorway to the window. Well, I ran over and opened the door. I stepped out into the dark. I nearly fell over a dead man. He lay across the doorway. I ran back for a light. The poor fellow had a deep cut in his throat. There was blood all over the hall. He lay on his back. His knees were pulled up. The man's mouth was wide open. I'll see him in my dreams. I screamed for the police. Then I must have fainted. The next I knew, a policeman was picking me up."

"Well, who was the murdered man?" asked Holmes.

"We don't know yet," said Lestrade. "You may see the body if you want. He is a tall man. He's very strong, not more than thirty. He is poorly dressed and sunburned. He doesn't seem to be a working man, though. A long knife was lying in the blood beside him. There was no name on his clothes. He had nothing in his pockets except an apple, some

string, a map of London, and a picture. Here's the picture."

The picture was a snapshot taken by a small camera. It showed a short, hairy, strong man. His face and body looked like those of an ape. Holmes studied the picture carefully.

"And what became of the bust?" he asked.

"We found out just before you came. It was in the yard of an empty house. It was broken to pieces like the others. I'm going round now to see it. Want to come along?"

"Yes. I want to take one look here first." He looked at the carpet and the window. "The fellow had long legs or he could really jump," he said. "It's quite a jump to the window."

The empty house was close by. The pieces of the bust lay scattered on the grass. Holmes picked some up and looked at them carefully. It looked to me as if he had found a clue.

"Well?" asked Lestrade.

"We have a long way to go," said Holmes. "Think of it! This cheap bust was worth more than a man's life. Let's remember that. Again, he did not break the bust in the house. He took it out here in the yard. The house was empty. He could have broken it there safely."

"He was scared. He'd just killed a man. He didn't

know just what he was doing," said Lestrade.

"Well, maybe. But look where this house is."

Lestrade looked around.

"It was an empty house. He knew nobody would be in the yard."

"Yes, but there's another empty house before this one. Why didn't he break it there? Every step meant danger to him."

"I give up," said Lestrade.

Holmes pointed to the street light above our heads.

"He could see what he was doing here. He couldn't over there. That's why he broke it here."

"Say! That's right," said Lestrade. "And Dr. Barnicot's bust was broken near his red lamp. Well, Holmes, what about it?"

"Just remember it now. We'll find something else later. What do you want to do now, Lestrade?"

"Well, we've got to find out who the dead man was. That should be easy. We find who he is. We find who his friends are. Then we can find out what he was doing on Pitt Street last night. We find out who met him. Then we've got the man who killed him. Don't you think so?"

"That sounds good. I wouldn't go at it just that way, though."

"What would you do?"

"Well, you do it your way. I'll do it mine. We'll

get together later on to tell you what we find."

"All right," said Lestrade.

"Watson, we have a hard day's work ahead of us. Lestrade, you meet us at Baker Street at six o'clock this evening. I'd like to keep this picture a while. You may have to go with us tonight. Good-bye and good luck."

Holmes and I first stopped at Harding Brothers. Holmes wanted to ask them about the bust. Mr. Harding wasn't there, though. The clerk was new. He could tell us nothing.

"Well, we can't have everything easy," said Holmes. "We'll come back later. I want to find out where Napoleon busts came from. Let's go see Mr. Hudson. Maybe he can help us."

We got there in about an hour. Mr. Hudson was a small fat man.

."Yes, sir," he said. "Right on my counter. I don't know why we have police. Yes, sir. I sold Dr. Barnicot his two statues. Where did I get them? What's that to do with it? Well, if you want to know, all right. They're from Gelder and Company. They have been well known for twenty years. How many did I have? Three. Two to Dr. Barnicot and one smashed on my own counter. Do I know the man in that picture? Let me see. No, I don't. Wait a minute. Yes, I do. Why, that's Joe. He's an Italian workman. Had him here in the shop. He left me last week. Haven't seen him since. No, I don't know where he came from nor where he went. He was gone two days before the bust was smashed."

"Well, that's some help," said Holmes. "We have this fellow Joe. He worked at Hudson's. He had something to do with the dead man. Let's go to Gelder and Co. They made the busts. We should get some help there."

We finally found Gelder and Co. Outside was a yard full of statues. Inside was a large room. Here about fifty workers were making statues. The manager came up and talked to us. He answered all Holmes' questions. They had made hundreds of the Napoleon busts. They made them in sets of six. Three had been sent to Morse Hudson a year or so before. The other three had gone to Harding Brothers. The six were just like the others. The manager didn't know why anybody would want to break them. The statues were cheap. They had two molds. One made one side of the head. The other made the second side. They put the two sides together to make the bust. The Italian workmen made them. They put the busts on a table to dry. Then they put them into a storeroom.

The manager did know the man in the picture. He got angry when he saw it.

"Ah, that one!" he cried. "Yes, I know him. We never have trouble here. Only once have the police been here. They came here for him. It was more than a year ago. He cut up another Italian. He came here to work with the police right on his heels. They caught him here. His name is Joe. I never knew his other name, but he was a good worker."

"Was he sent to jail?"

"Yes. The other fellow didn't die. So Joe got off with a year. I guess he's out by now. He hasn't been around here. His cousin works here. He could tell you where he is."

"No, no," cried Holmes. "Not a word to his cousin. I don't want him to know. Could you tell me when Joe was arrested?"

"I can tell you when we paid him last." The manager turned the pages of his book. "Yes, here it is. We paid him on May 20. He was arrested a little after that."

"Thank you," said Holmes. We turned to go.

We didn't get any lunch until late afternoon. Then we went on to Harding Brothers again. Mr. Harding was a small, snappy little man.

"Yes," he said. "I've read about the case in the papers. Mr. Harker bought the Napoleon bust from us. We got three busts from Gelder and Co. We

71

sold them all. To whom? Oh, I can find out for you. Let me look at our sales book. Here we are. One went to Mr. Harker. One went to Mr. Joseph Brown. The third went to a Mr. Sandford. Here are their addresses if you want them. No, I have never seen this man in the picture. Do we have any Italian workers? Yes, we have a few. Yes, they could look at this sales book if they wanted to. Well, let me know if you find anything out."

Holmes made a few notes while Mr. Harding talked. I could see that he was pleased. We hurried off to meet Lestrade. He was waiting for us at Baker Street.

"Well," he asked, "what luck, Mr. Holmes?"

"We've had a busy day. We know where the busts came from and where they went."

"The busts!" cried Lestrade. "Well, you have your own ways, Mr. Holmes. I think I've done better than you. I found out who the dead man was."

"You don't say so?"

"And I know why he was killed."

"Fine!"

"Detective Hill at Scotland Yard knows the Italians well. He knew the dead man right away. He was Pete Venucci. He was one of the greatest cutthroats in London. He belonged to one of the Italian gangs. If you don't do what they say, they kill you. Pete was probably after this fellow. He carried the picture so he'd get the right man. He followed him. He saw him go into this house. He waited outside. He went after him, and he himself was killed in the fight. How's that, Mr. Sherlock Holmes?"

Holmes clapped his hands.

"Good, Lestrade. Very good. But how about the Napoleon busts?"

"The busts! Get them out of your head. What do we care about the busts? We want the killer. And I'm close to him."

"Well, what will you do next?"

"That's easy. I'll go down to the Italian part of town and find this fellow Joe. Then I'll arrest him. Do you want to go along?"

"I think not. I have an easier way. I'll just make you a bet. You come with me tonight, and I'll catch him for you."

"Where the Italians live?"

"No. At the home of a man named Joseph Brown. You go with me tonight, Lestrade. If we don't get him, I'll go with you tomorrow. How's that? Now I think we could get a little sleep. I want to leave about eleven o'clock. We won't be back before morning. You eat with us, Lestrade. Then you can get a nap in here until we start. Watson, call up for a messenger boy. I want to send a letter right away."

Holmes spent the evening looking through old newspapers. When he got through he was smiling. I knew he had found what he wanted, but he said nothing. I didn't know what it was all about. I did know that Holmes thought the man would try to get at the other two busts. One was at the home of this Joseph Brown. The other was Mr. Sanford's. I knew Holmes hoped to catch the man breaking in. I wasn't surprised when he told me to take my gun along.

A cab was at the door at eleven. We drove to the other side of town. Then we got out and walked. Finally Holmes pointed to a house. The people who lived there were in bed. Everything was dark but a little light over the doorway. A big wooden fence ran around the house. Holmes led us behind the fence.

"We'll wait here," he said. "I'm glad it isn't raining. We can smoke. We may have to wait a while."

But we didn't have long to wait. We heard no sound, but suddenly the yard gate swung open. Someone went running up the path. He was short and dark. He ran fast, like an ape. We saw him go past the little light. Then he was gone. A minute later we heard a window opening. Then it was quiet again. We saw a flash of light in the room. A bit later we saw light from another room.

"Let's get to the window," whispered Lestrade. "We'll catch him coming out."

But the man was out again before we could move. He carried something white under his arm. He looked around. The street was quiet. He turned his back to us. He laid the white thing on the ground. We heard a sharp tap, then something breaking. He never heard us as we crept close to him. With a leap like a tiger Holmes was on his back. Lestrade and I each grabbed an arm. In a minute we had the handcuffs on him. We rolled him over. It was the man in the picture—the man called Joe.

Holmes didn't even look at the man. He was over on the doorstep. He was looking at the pieces of the broken Napoleon. Carefully he looked at each piece. Then the lights went on in the house. A big, heavy man came out.

"Mr. Joseph Brown?" asked Holmes.

"Yes, sir. And I guess you are Sherlock Holmes. I got the letter you sent by messenger this morning. I did just what you told me. We locked every door and just waited. I'm glad you got the man. Won't you come in and have a drink?"

But Lestrade wanted to get Joe into jail right

away. So we called a cab and rode back to town. Joe wouldn't say a word. Once when I got my hand close to him, he snapped at it like a wolf. He had nothing on him but a long ugly knife. We saw some dried blood on the blade.

"That's all right," said Lestrade as we left him. "Detective Hill will know this fellow. You'll find out I was right about the gang. I want to thank you, though, Mr. Holmes. I still don't know how you figured him out."

"Well, it's a little late now. And the case isn't finished at all. You come around tomorrow at six o'clock. I think I'll have another surprise for you."

We met again next evening. Lestrade had found out something about our man. His name really was Joe. No one knew his other name. He was well known among the Italians. He had been a good worker. He had made an honest living for some time. Then he went bad. He'd been in jail twice. Once he'd been in for stealing. The second time he'd been in for stabbing a man. He could speak English well. He would say nothing about the busts. The police had found out he could have made them himself. That's what he had been doing for Gelder and Co. Holmes listened to all this. At last he got up. His eye grew brighter. The bell had rung downstairs. A minute later we heard a step on the stairs.

An old red-faced man with whiskers came in. In his right hand he carried a bag. He put the bag on the table.

"Is Mr. Sherlock Holmes here?"

Holmes smiled. "Mr. Sandford, aren't you?"

"Yes, sir. I'm a little late. The train was slow. You wrote me about a bust of Napoleon?"

"I did."

"I have your letter here. It says you'll pay me ten pounds for it. Is that right?"

"That's right."

"I was surprised about the letter. How did you know I had the bust?"

"Mr. Harding had your name. He gave it to me."

"Oh, I see. Did he tell you what I paid for it?"

"No, he did not."

"Well, I'm not rich, but I am honest. I didn't pay much for the bust. You should know that before you pay me ten pounds."

"I gave you that price. I'll stick to it. Ten pounds it is."

"Well, fine. I brought the bust with me, as you asked. Here it is."

He opened his bag. He put a bust of Napoleon on the table. Holmes gave him a paper to sign and gave him the ten pounds.

When he was gone Holmes moved quickly. First

he laid a clean white cloth on the table. Then he put the bust on the cloth. He picked up a hammer and hit Napoleon on top of the head. The bust broke into pieces. Holmes bent over them. He let out a yell. He held up one piece. A round dark thing like a plum was stuck in it.

"Gentlemen," said Holmes, "I want you to take a look at the famous black pearl of the Borgias."

Lestrade and I were quiet for a minute. Then we both clapped our hands like children. Holmes laughed.

"Yes, gentlemen," he said, "it is the most famous pearl in the world. It was stolen from the Prince of Colonna's bedroom. You remember when it was stolen, Lestrade. The London police tried for months to find it. The Princess' maid was an Italian. She had a brother in London. Her name was Lucy Venucci. Her brother was Pete Venucci, who was killed the other night. I found out that the pearl was stolen two days before Joe was arrested. Joe was arrested for stabbing, you remember. He ran to Gelder and Co., where he worked. He was making the six Napoleon busts then. Joe had the pearl. He may have stolen it from Pete Venucci. He may have been in it with Pete.

"Anyway, he had the pearl. The police were after him. He had only a few minutes to hide it. If he didn't, the police would find it on him. Six Napoleon busts were drying on the table. One of them was still soft. Joe made a small hole in the bust. He dropped in the pearl. He covered the hole. It was a good hiding place. No one could find it. But Joe went to jail for a year. While he was there the six busts were sold. He couldn't tell which bust held the pearl. So he had to find them and break them open. His cousin worked at Gelder. He got him to find out where the six busts had gone. The cousin just looked into Gelder's sales book and found out. Gelder had sent three to Morse Hudson and three to Harding Brothers. So Joe got himself a job at Morse Hudson's. There he tracked down three of them. One was still at Hudson's. Two were at Dr. Barnicot's. But the pearl wasn't in those three. Next he found out what happened to Harding's three busts. One was at Mr. Harker's house. There he ran into Pete Venucci. Pete must have been following him. So he killed Pete."

"Why did Pete carry his picture? Pete knew him."

"Pete must have lost track of him. He used the picture to ask people if they had seen Joe. After the murder I figured Joe would hurry. He wanted to stay ahead of the police. He wanted that pearl badly. It wasn't in Harker's statue. That left only two. Mr. Brown lived in London. Mr. Sandford didn't. I figured he'd try Brown's house first. I knew he was after the pearl. I knew that when you told me Pete's name was Venucci. I remembered the Princess' maid's name was Venucci. When the pearl wasn't there, I knew it was in Sandford's statue. So I bought it. And there it is."

We sat quiet for a minute.

"Well," said Lestrade. "I've seen you work on a great many cases, Mr. Holmes. But this was really a slick one. We're not jealous over at Scotland Yard. We're proud of you. Everybody there will be glad to shake your hand."

"Thank you," said Holmes. "Thank you. All right, Watson. We have another case coming up. Get out the papers. Good-bye, Lestrade. I'll be glad to help you any time. Come see us again."

The Adventure of the Empty House

IT was in 1895 that London was shocked by the murder of Ronald Adair. A part of the story came out in the papers. But the whole story has never been told. Only now, ten years later, can I tell it.

The crime was interesting enough. But the crime was nothing to the other things that happened at the same time.

Four years before, on April 24, 1891, Sherlock Holmes had come to my office. It was then I first learned that the cleverest and most powerful criminal in the world was out to get Holmes. It had taken Holmes years to corner the master criminal—Professor James Moriarty. One more week and he would have Moriarty and the whole gang. Moriarty warned him—quit or die with him. Holmes laughed at him.

The next day Holmes was almost killed in an accident. The same day a pile of bricks from a roof missed him by a foot or two. That night three men tried to finish him. Holmes escaped with badly broken knuckles. But to stay longer in London was sure death.

We did escape. We made our way slowly to Switzerland. But before we arrived, Holmes had bad news from Scotland Yard. The gang was caught, but Moriarty had escaped. Holmes knew what that meant. Moriarty was after him.

We went out walking one day to the Reichenbach Fall. We stood at the edge of the rocky cliff, looking down hundreds of feet below. Just then a boy came from the hotel, looking for me. A woman was sick. Would I come? Holmes told me to go ahead. He would wait for me. But when I reached the hotel, there was no sick woman. No one had sent for me. In a minute I knew the truth. Moriarty!

I rushed back to the cliff. There was no one there. Holmes' walking stick lay near the edge. Then I saw his cigarette case. Inside was a note to me. I knew what a fool I'd been. Holmes had guessed everything when the boy had come. And he let me go back so I'd be out of danger! He knew the end had come, he wrote. He wasn't sorry. Moriarty would be there any minute. But one thing was sure. Professor Moriarty was going over with him.

The ground near the edge of the cliff told the story. Holmes' footprints were clear. Moriarty's prints came up to them. The deep marks told the story of that last desperate fight. No footprints came back from the edge. Locked in each other's arms they had plunged to the sharp rocks far below.

I went back to London with a heavy heart. The world had lost its greatest detective and I my best friend.

Though Holmes was gone, I kept up my interest in crimes. I read the story of every one in the papers. I even tried to use Holmes' methods to figure them out. But there was only one Sherlock Holmes. I just could not do it.

I became interested in the murder of Ronald Adair, a strange case. Ronald Adair was the second son of a fine old family. The mother had come to London with her son Ronald and daughter Hilda. The mother had bad eyes and was going to a famous London doctor. The family lived together at 427 Park Lane. Ronald had no enemies and no very bad habits. He had been engaged, but that had been broken off a few months before. He and the girl were still good friends. And still, between ten and eleven-twenty on the night of March 30, 1895, Ronald Adair was unexpectedly murdered.

Young Adair liked to play cards. And he played a lot. But he never played for more than he could afford. He belonged to three famous card clubs in London. Before and after dinner on the day he died, he had played bridge. Three men had been playing with him. They were a Mr. Murray, Sir John Hardy, and Colonel Moran. They agreed the game had been pretty even. Adair might have lost five pounds, but not more. He had plenty of his own money. Such a small loss didn't matter to him. He had played often before, but he was a careful player. Usually he won. Only a week before, he and Colonel Moran had won four hundred and twenty pounds in one afternoon.

On the evening of the crime, he came home at ten o'clock. His mother and sister were out visiting a relative. The servant said she heard him come in and go to the front room, second floor. She had lit a fire in the fireplace and had opened the window. The fire had been smoking badly. No other sound came from the room until eleven-twenty. Mrs. Adair and Hilda had come back then. They stopped at Ronald's room to say good night. The door was locked. They knocked and called but, no answer. Mrs. Adair got help and broke the door open. Ronald Adair lay near the table with a bullet in his head. There was no gun in the room. On the table lay neat little piles of money. There was also a sheet of paper. On this were names of friends and numbers. It looked as if young Adair had been figuring out his card winnings.

No one knew why he locked the door. Perhaps the killer had done this and escaped through the window. But the window was twenty feet above the ground. A big flower bed was under the window. And there wasn't a mark on the ground or flowers. Adair must have locked that door. But how was he killed? No one could have climbed to the window without leaving a mark.

Suppose a man had shot him through the window. But Park Lane is a busy street. There is a cab stand nearby. No one had heard a shot. And yet there was the dead man. As I have said, he had no enemies. No one had touched the money.

I thought about the case all day. I just couldn't figure out how it happened. In the evening I walked over to Park Lane. A few people were standing around talking and looking up at the house. One man was pointing to the window and telling what he thought about the murder. I listened to him for a while. His ideas sounded pretty silly to me.

I turned away. As I did, I bumped into a little old man who was standing behind me. I knocked some books out of his arms. I picked them up and put them back in his arms. I tried to tell him I was sorry, but he snarled at me and walked off. In a minute his curved back and white whiskers were gone in the crowd.

My visit to No. 427 Park Lane didn't help me much. A low wall and railing ran next to the sidewalk. It was about five feet high. Anyone could climb it and enter the garden. But there was no way to reach the window from the garden. I gave it up and went back to my office. About five minutes later, the maid said a man wanted to see me. To my surprise, it was the old man I'd bumped into. He had his books under his arm.

"You're surprised to see me, sir," he said in a strange croaking voice.

"Yes, I am."

"Well, sir, I saw you go into this house. I thought I had not been very polite to you. I just want to tell you I'm sorry. I didn't mean to be rough."

"It doesn't matter at all."

"Well, sir, I'm a neighbor. I have a little book store on the corner. Do you buy books? I sell them very cheap. These five I have would just fill up your empty shelf over there."

I turned my head to look. When I looked back, Sherlock Holmes was smiling at me across the table. I rose to my feet. My eyes popped out. And then,

the only time in my life, I fainted. When I came to, my collar was loose and Holmes was bending over me.

"My dear Watson," he said. "I am sorry. I didn't think—"

I grabbed him by the arms.

"Holmes!" I cried. "Is it really you? Are you really alive? How could you be?"

"Wait a minute," he said. "Are you all right? Do you feel well? I shouldn't have done that."

"Oh, I'm all right. But, Holmes, I can't believe my eyes. Good heavens! To think that you—you are here!" Again I grabbed him by the arms. I could feel the steel muscles of his thin arms. "Well, you're not a ghost, anyway. Holmes, you don't know how happy I am to see you. Sit down and tell me how on earth you got away from Moriarty."

He sat down and lit a cigarette. He was dressed in the dusty old coat of the book seller. On the table lay the white hair and books. Holmes looked thinner and keener than ever. But his face was pale and tired.

"I'm glad to stretch out, Watson," he said. "I've had to look about a foot shorter than I am. Now, about my story. We have a hard night's work in front of us. Suppose I tell about myself later."

"Holmes, I can't wait. Tell me now."

"Will you go with me tonight?"

"Whenever you want and wherever you want."

"Good. This is like old times again. We can eat before we go. But now about Moriarty and the cliff. I never went over the cliff."

"Didn't go over it?"

"No, Watson. My note to you was real enough. I thought it was all over. Moriarty came down the path to the cliff. I was standing at the very edge. He had no gun. But suddenly he rushed me. He wrapped his powerful arms around me. He knew it was the end for him but he wanted to get me, too. We stumbled around on the edge. You know I am pretty good at jiu-jitsu, or Japanese wrestling. I slipped through his grip, and threw him over. He clawed the air with both hands, but he couldn't help himself. With a horrible scream he went over the edge. I saw him fall for a long way. Then he hit a rock and bounced off. Finally he hit the water far below."

"But the tracks," I cried. "I saw, with my own eyes. Two went down the path and none came back."

"This is what happened. When Professor Moriarty went over, I thought for a minute. Moriarty was not the only man who wanted me dead. Scotland Yard had caught only the small fry of his gang. There were at least three men who would give anything to get me. They were all dangerous men. One of the three would get me. But if the world thought I was dead, these men would dare anything. I could pick them off one by one. Then I could come back.

"I stood up and looked at the rocky wall behind me. Everyone thinks that wall is perfectly smooth rock. It isn't. There are a few tiny foot holds. I made up my mind to risk it. That was a climb, Watson! One slip and I was gone. The water roared below me. Sometimes I'd think I heard Moriarty's voice again, screaming at me. More than once the grass I held pulled out. Several times my foot slipped from the wet rock. But I kept going up. At last I reached a narrow ledge. There I lay unseen. And from there I watched when you and the police came back.

"Then you were sure Moriarty and I had gone over together. You left to go back to the hotel. I thought my little adventure was over. Suddenly a big rock came from the very top of the cliff above me. It hit the path and bounced over the edge. At first I thought it was an accident. I turned and looked upward. I saw a man's head over the edge. Then another rock hit the ledge on which I lay. Then I knew. Moriarty had not come alone. A pal—and one look told me how dangerous he was—

was there. He had seen me pitch his friend to his death. He had watched me crawl up the side of the cliff.

"I didn't stay there long to think it over, Watson. Again I saw that face look over at me. More stones were coming. I scrambled back down. I don't know how I ever made it. It was a hundred times harder getting down than coming up. Halfway down I slipped. I was lucky. Torn and bleeding I landed on the path. I made ten miles that night, in the dark. A week later I was in Italy.

"Only one other man knew I was alive—my brother, Mycroft. I couldn't let you know, Watson. Everyone had to think I was dead. Several times in the last three years, I've started to write to you. But I was afraid you might make a slip and give me away. I didn't even speak to you on the street to-night. I was in great danger even then. I had to let Mycroft know I was alive because I needed money. I traveled for two years in China. And you may have read about the explorer Sigerson. Sigerson and Sherlock Holmes are the same. I've been all over the world these past three years. At last I found out that only one of my enemies is in London. So I decided to come back. The Ronald Adair mystery made me hurry. I have reasons to be very much interested in the case.

"So I came back to London. I went to Baker Street from the station. Mycroft has kept my rooms as they were. So, Watson, at two o'clock today I was back in my old armchair in my old room. All I needed was my old friend sitting across from me."

That was the story Holmes told me that evening. I couldn't have believed it from anyone else.

"We have a job tonight, Watson," he said.

"What is it, Holmes?" I asked eagerly.

But he would tell me nothing about it.

"You will hear and see enough before morning," he said. "We can talk of other things until half-past nine. Then we start the adventure of the empty house."

It was like old times. At nine-thirty we were off. My gun was in my pocket, and Holmes sat silent beside me in the cab. Someone was in for trouble.

I thought at first we were going to Baker Street. But we went on and on. At last we left the cab to walk. At each corner Holmes looked to see if we were being followed. In ten minutes I was lost, but Holmes knew London perfectly. At last we came to a narrow street. On both sides were dark old houses. We slipped through one of the gates and went up the steps. Holmes opened the back door with a key. We went in together. He closed the door behind us.

The house was pitch dark. I could tell it was empty. There were no rugs on the floors. When I touched the wall, I felt strips of torn wallpaper. Holmes' cold thin fingers closed on my wrist. He led me down the hall. Here he turned suddenly to the right. We were now in a square empty room. Some light came in from the street outside, but the corners were dark. The window was thick with dust. Holmes put his hand on my shoulder. His lips were close to my ear.

"Do you know where we are?" he whispered.

"Why, that's Baker Street," I said, looking outside.

"It is. There are my rooms, across the street."

"But why are we here?"

"Because we can see the house so well. Get closer to the window and look out. Don't let anyone see you. Now look up at my rooms."

I crawled to the window and looked out carefully. As I looked at Holmes' windows I fell back in surprise. A strong light was burning in his room. A man's shadow showed black and clear through the window. I would have sworn it was Sherlock Holmes, sitting in his chair. I was so surprised I reached out to make sure he was with me. He was shaking with laughter.

"Well?" he said.

"Good heavens!" I cried. "How did you do it?"

"It really is like me, isn't it?" ,

"It would fool me."

"A French artist did it for me. It's wax. I fixed it up this afternoon."

"But why?"

"Because I wanted someone to think I was there."

"You thought someone was watching your rooms?"

"I *knew* someone was watching."

"Who?"

"My old enemies, Watson. The men whose leader lies in the Reichenbach Fall. Only they know I am still alive. Sooner or later they knew I'd come back to my rooms. They've watched for three years. This morning they saw me."

"How do you know?"

"Because I spotted their man. A fellow named Parker—a small time killer. I'm not worried about him. I am worried about the man behind him. That man is the pal of Moriarty. He's the man who pushed the rocks down at me. And he's the most dangerous man in London. That man is after me tonight, Watson. But he doesn't know we are after *him*."

I began to get the idea. The shadow in Holmes' window was bait. We were the hunters. We watched the people pass on the street. Holmes never moved once. He looked closely at everyone who passed. It was a cold night. The wind whistled in the street. Most people had on heavy coats. I thought I saw the same man pass several times. I watched two men in the doorway of a house up the street. I started to point them out to Holmes, but he just put his finger to his lips. Holmes began to get uneasy after a while. His plans were not going right. By midnight the street was nearly empty. He began to walk up and down in the room. I looked across Baker Street again. I got another surprise. I grabbed Holmes' arm and pointed.

"The shadow has moved!" I cried.

The back of the head was now turned toward us.

"Of course it has moved," he said. "Do you think I'm a fool, Watson? The sharpest man in Europe is watching that shadow. Do you suppose I could fool him if it didn't? We have been in this room two hours. Mrs. Hudson has moved that dummy eight times. She works it from the front so her shadow doesn't show. Ah!"

He leaned forward. The street was empty. The two men might still be in the doorway. I could no longer see them. Everything was still and dark. Suddenly Holmes pulled me into the blackest corner of the room. He put his hand over my lips. And still the street was dark and empty.

But then I heard what he had already heard. A low sound came to my ears. But not from Baker Street! It came from the back of the very house in which we were! A door opened and shut. Then footsteps came softly down the hall. Holmes flattened himself against the wall. I did the same, getting hold of my gun. In the darkness I saw a man in the doorway. He stood there a moment. Then he crawled into the room. He was about three yards from us. I got set for him. Then suddenly it dawned on me. He didn't know we were in the room! He almost touched us as he passed. He softly raised the window about six inches. Then he got on his knees. The light from the street shone on his face. He was terribly excited. His eyes shone like stars and he bit his lips. He was an older man, with a high, thin nose. His forehead was high and he had a thick moustache. A high silk hat was pushed back on his head. A stiff dress shirt showed over his coat. His face was dark, with deep lines in it.

I thought he had a stick in his hand. But when he laid it on the floor it gave a clang, like metal. Then he got something out of his coat pocket. He bent over it and then we heard a loud, sharp click. He had set a spring of some kind, it seemed. Now he bent forward and threw his weight on some lever. There was a long grinding noise, then another click.

He straightened up. I saw what he held in his hands. It was a strange gun of some kind. He opened it, put something in, and snapped it shut. He laid the barrel of the gun on the window sill. I saw his eye shine as he aimed at the shadow in the window. For a moment he didn't move. Then he pulled the trigger. There was a strange loud whizzing sound. Glass fell to the sidewalk across the street. Holmes jumped like a tiger on the man's back. Down the killer went, flat on his face. But he was up in a moment. He grabbed Holmes by the throat. Then I let him have the butt of my gun on his head. He dropped to the floor. I threw myself on top of him. I heard Holmes blow his police whistle. We heard running feet on the sidewalk. Two policemen and a plain-clothes detective rushed in through the front door.

"Is that you, Lestrade?" said Holmes.

"Yes, Mr. Holmes. I took the job myself. It's good to see you back in London, sir."

We all got to our feet. Our prisoner was breathing hard. A policeman had him by each arm. Lestrade lit a lantern. We looked at the man we had caught. He was a big strong man, with cruel eyes. He looked only at Holmes. Surprise and hate were in his face. "You fiend," he kept saying. "You clever, clever fiend."

"Ah, Colonel," said Holmes. "I'm glad to see you. I haven't seen you since you pushed rocks down at me at Reichenbach Fall."

The colonel just kept looking at Holmes. "You clever, clever fiend," he said again.

"This man is Colonel Sebastian Moran," said Holmes. "He is the best big game hunter of the British Army in India. Nobody ever broke your record for shooting tigers, eh, Colonel?"

The fierce old man said nothing. He just looked with hate at Holmes. He looked almost like a tiger himself.

"I'm surprised you fell for it, Colonel," said Holmes.

Colonel Moran jumped at Holmes with an angry snarl. The policemen dragged him back.

"You did surprise me," said Holmes. "I didn't know you were going to use this house. I thought you'd shoot from the street. Lestrade and his men were waiting there."

Colonel Moran turned to Lestrade. "Go on and arrest me," he said. "I don't have to listen to him. If Scotland Yard wants me, take me away."

"That's all right with me," said Lestrade. "Anything else before we go, Mr. Holmes?"

Holmes had picked up Moran's powerful air gun. He looked at it carefully.

"A wonderful gun," he said. "No noise and great power. I know the German gun maker who made it for Moriarty. I've known about it for years. This is the first time I've touched it. Look at it, Lestrade. And don't forget the bullets that fit it."

"We'll do that, Mr. Holmes. Anything else?"

"What are you going to charge him with, Lestrade?"

"Charge him with? Why, with trying to murder Sherlock Holmes."

"No, Lestrade. Leave me out of it. You take the credit for the case. Yes, Lestrade, I take off my hat to you. You got him. You've been very clever and daring."

"Got him? Got whom, Mr. Holmes?"

"The man Scotland Yard wants. Colonel Moran, who shot Ronald Adair with an air gun. The man who shot through the open window at 427 Park Lane on the thirtieth of last month. That's the charge, Lestrade. Now, Watson, if that broken window won't make my room too cold, let's go home."

Our old rooms were the same as they had been. Mrs. Hudson was waiting for us. And the dummy was there. It was a model of my friend, and looked exactly like him. It stood on a table with an old robe of Holmes' over the shoulders.

"Are you sure you followed my instructions

exactly as I told you, Mrs. Hudson?" said Holmes.

"Yes, sir. I came in on my knees so no one could see me. I moved it very carefully every fifteen minutes."

"Good. You did very well. Did you see where the bullet went?"

"Yes, sir. I'm afraid it ruined the wax dummy. It went right through the head. It flattened against the wall. I picked it up on the rug. Here it is."

Holmes held it out to me. "Look at that, Watson. A soft-nosed revolver bullet. Who would guess that came from an air gun? All right, Mrs. Hudson. Thank you. And now, Watson, sit down."

He looked at the broken dummy. "The old tiger killer is still a good shot. Right through the head. He was the best shot in India. Did you ever hear of him?"

"No, I didn't."

"Well, you didn't hear of Moriarty, either. And he was one of the smartest men in the world. Moran was the son of a famous English family. Went to the best schools—Eton and Oxford. Got into the Army and went to India. Wrote some books on big game hunting. He was long the second most danger-ous man in London."

"It's too bad. He could have been a great man."

"Yes, he could. He had iron nerve. They still

tell a story in India about him. He crawled down a drain pipe after a wounded man-eating tiger. Well, anyway, he went wrong. India got too hot to hold him. He came to London and soon had a bad name here. Professor Moriarty got interested in him. Moran soon became the No. 2 man. Moriarty used him only on high class jobs. Do you remember the death of Mrs. Stewart, in 1887? No? Well, I'm sure Moran was in back of that. Moran was well covered up. When the Moriarty gang was caught they had nothing on Moran. Do you remember when I came to see you three years ago? I closed the shutters on your office windows. I was afraid of the air gun then. I knew the best shot in the world would pull the trigger. He followed us to Switzerland with Moriarty. It was he who nearly got me as I lay on the ledge at the Reichenbach Fall.

"While I was away I watched the papers. I hoped he'd do something so I could get him. So long as he was free, in London, he could get me. What could I do? I couldn't shoot him. I couldn't prove anything against him. So I could do nothing. I watched the papers. Then came the death of Ronald Adair. My chance had come. Who could have done it but Moran? He had played cards with Adair. He followed him home. He shot him through the open window. I knew that's what happened. I came back. Their man saw me. I knew he'd tell Moran right away. Moran knew why I was back. He would try to get me *at once*. So I set up the dummy for him. I warned Scotland Yard. I picked the house across the street to watch from. I didn't know he'd pick it to shoot from. Is that everything, Watson?"

"No, Holmes," I said. "Why did Moran murder Ronald Adair?"

"Ah, Watson, there we may need to do some guessing."

"Well, how do you guess that one?"

"It's not very hard. You remember Colonel Moran and Adair won a good bit of money playing together. Moran is a card sharp. I've long known that he cheats. I'm sure Adair found it out. He must have warned him to quit playing and give back the money. Moran made his living by playing cards. So he killed Adair. Adair was figuring out how much to pay back himself when the bullet hit him. He had locked the door so his family wouldn't ask about the money on the table. Is that a good guess?"

"I'm sure you've hit it right."

"We'll soon find out. Colonel Moran will trouble us no more. The famous German air gun will go to Scotland Yard. Again Sherlock Holmes will be free to work on the mysteries of London."

About the Author (Editor's Note)

You may be interested in the man who wrote the Sherlock Holmes stories. He called himself Dr. Watson, but that was not his name. He was really Sir Arthur Conan Doyle.

He was born in 1859, in Edinburgh, Scotland, of Irish parents. His grandfather, his father, and his uncles were artists. Arthur himself wrote a book and drew the pictures for it while he was still a boy.

The Doyles did not have much money, but the boy had a good education. He went to Edinburgh University to become a doctor. Doyle had to stop school several times to earn money to go on. One of his teachers at Edinburgh was a Dr. Joseph Bell. This Dr. Bell became the Sherlock Holmes of Doyle's stories.

As part of his university work, Doyle sailed as the ship doctor on a whaling boat. When he got out of school he made another trip, this time to West Africa. But he needed money and decided he had better open his doctor's office. In 1882 he did, at Southsea, England. He married in 1885.

He had a hard time. He was poor and the patients came slowly. So he read books to pass the time, and, in the evenings, he began to write stories himself. Soon the magazines began to take some of his stories. He made enough money to get by.

Doyle had read Edgar Allan Poe's stories. Best of all he liked Poe's detective stories—"The Murders in the Rue Morgue," "The Mystery of Marie Roget," and "The Purloined Letter." The time was just right to sell short, exciting stories in England. England had built many railroads, and thousands of people were traveling every day. These people wanted short stories to read on the trains. They wanted stories they could finish on one trip. Doyle saw that clearly.

He had never forgotten his teacher, Dr. Joseph Bell. He remembered how clever Dr. Bell had been. Once, for example, a man had come to Bell for help. The talk went something like this:

"You've been in the army," said Bell.

"Yes, sir."

"You haven't been out long."

"No, sir, just a short time."

"You were in a Scottish regiment, weren't you?"

"Yes, sir."

"You were a non-com officer."

"Yes, sir."

"You were at Barbados."

"Yes, sir."

Bell explained how he guessed these things. The man had been very polite, but he had kept his hat on. Soldiers keep their hats on even when talking to officers. The man would learn to take off his hat after he had been out of the army a while, so Bell knew he had just come out. The man acted as if he were used to giving orders, so Bell guessed he had been an officer. He could tell from his voice he was a Scotsman. The man had a kind of sickness which people get in the West Indies. There was an army post in Barbados, so Bell guessed he had come from there.

Another time Bell brought a patient before the class. He called one of the students to come forward.

"What's the matter with this man?" he asked.

The student was nervous. He had seen the man limp. He reached toward the man to find out what was the matter.

"No!" cried Bell. "Don't touch him. Use your eyes to find out."

The student made a guess. He thought something was wrong with the man's hip.

"No," said Bell. "Anybody can see he limps. But his hip is all right. It's his feet. Look at his shoes. He has cut the leather open. He limps because he has corns. But he is not here for sore feet. Look at his face. This man drinks too much. Anybody can see that. And look here!"

He pointed to the man's side pocket. Everyone could see the neck of a bottle of liquor sticking out. Dr. Bell did things like this again and again.

Why not, thought Doyle, write short detective stories like Poe's and make Dr. Bell the hero? He invented Dr. Watson and Sherlock Holmes and brought them together in a longer story called *A Study in Scarlet*, in 1886. He sent the story to many publishers. They sent it back again and again. At last one man gave him twenty-five pounds (about $125) for it. Sherlock Holmes did not become popular quickly. Two years later an American magazine asked Doyle to write another Holmes story. He wrote "The Sign of the Four." It was printed in the United States and in England. Then other magazines grew interested. The *Strand Magazine* asked Doyle to write twelve short Holmes stories. So Doyle started the short stories. Before he started them, he made a trip to Berlin. On the way he met a friend. This friend advised him to become an eye specialist. Doyle thought it was a good idea. He went to Vienna and studied. When he finished he opened an office in London. Doyle came in every morning at ten and waited for patients to ring the bell. But the bell never rang. He had lots of time to write. He began to turn out the Holmes stories that made him famous.

The first one was "A Scandal in Bohemia," in the *Strand Magazine*. The editor liked it and paid $500 for it. He asked Doyle to write a Sherlock Holmes story for each month. Soon thousands waited eagerly for the next story to come. Sherlock Holmes became known all over the world, and Arthur Conan Doyle became a famous writer.

While Doyle was busy digging up new puzzles for Sherlock Holmes to solve, Mrs. Doyle got sick. So Doyle moved his family to Switzerland, where the climate was better. He was worried about his wife's health, and he just could not keep on thinking up new plots. He decided to kill off Sherlock Holmes.

In Switzerland he saw the falls of Reichenbach. There, he thought, was the place to drop Sherlock Holmes! So he wrote "The Final Problem." In this story he brought Professor Moriarty and Sherlock Holmes together at the edge of the falls. He ended the story with Holmes' and Moriarty's deaths.

Everybody thought, of course, that was the end of Sherlock Holmes. People all over the world wrote Doyle angry letters. Some were from women who were very angry. Many had hoped to marry Sherlock Holmes someday! One started her letter with "You Beast!"

Doyle was almost ready to bring Holmes back to life in 1902. He wrote "The Hound of the Baskervilles" but said the story had happened before Holmes was killed. Then he wrote "The Adventure of the Empty House" for *Collier's Magazine* in the United States and for the *Strand Magazine* in England in 1903. You will remember that in this book the two stories, "The Final Problem" and "The Empty House," have been put together as one story.

Readers of the Holmes stories were glad to have their hero back. On the day the *Strand Magazine* came out, long lines of people waited to buy it. Some thought the new stories were not so good as the early ones. Doyle tells that he was once talking to a sailor about Sherlock Holmes' return.

"I think, sir," said the sailor, "when Holmes fell over that cliff, he may not have killed himself, but he was never quite the same man afterwards."

Doyle himself knew the first stories were the best. He wanted to quit, but his readers just would not stand for it. Doyle did not want to be remembered because of Sherlock Holmes. He thought his other books were much better.

Sir Arthur Conan Doyle wrote as though he were Watson himself. But he was quite a Sherlock Holmes, too. He once worked on a real murder case for eighteen years. This was the famous Oscar Slater case.

A woman named Gilchrist lived in Glasgow, Scotland. Miss Gilchrist liked jewelry and kept some in her home. She had always been afraid of burglars. A Mr. Adams lived in the flat below her. She had told Mr. Adams if she were ever being robbed, she would rap on her floor three times for help.

A few days before Christmas, 1908, Miss Gilchrist sent her maid, Helen Lambie, out to buy a newspaper. A little later Adams heard three knocks on the floor above. He did not even stop to put on his glasses. He rushed up the stairs just as the maid was coming back. When they got to the door, a man walked out. They did not look at him closely, but hurried inside. There lay Miss Gilchrist, dead. A diamond brooch was missing.

People all over Scotland were interested in the case. The police picked up the trail of a man named Oscar Slater. Slater had left Glasgow on Christmas Day. He had pawned a diamond brooch and was on his way to New York. The New York Police held him. Adams, Helen Lambie, and a girl who had been in the street went to New York. Helen Lambie said Slater was the man who had come out of the door. The girl said she had seen Slater run into the street. Adams was not sure. Slater agreed to come back to Scotland for trial.

He was tried in Edinburgh and found guilty. The sentence was death. At the last moment the death sentence was changed to life in prison.

Doyle got interested in the case. He showed that the brooch Slater pawned was his own. He proved that Helen Lambie could not have told if the man was Slater or not. He showed also that the police had talked the girl into saying she had seen Slater. At last he got the case opened again. Slater got out of prison after serving eighteen years.

People sometimes brought cases to Doyle to solve. He tried to solve them as he thought Holmes would have done. Once a man disappeared from a London hotel. Before he did, he took out about $200 which he had in a bank. The police thought someone might have robbed and killed him. The man had gone to a show and had come back about ten o'clock at night. No one saw him leave. The man in the next room said he had heard him moving around during the night. The police could find out nothing.

A week later the case came to Doyle. Where was the man?

Doyle wrote back that the man was in either Glasgow or Edinburgh. The police later found the man had gone to Edinburgh. How did he know? This is the way Doyle got the answer:

Doyle thought the man wanted to disappear because he had taken his money from the bank. He had gone during the night. But London hotels close their doors about midnight and put the porter on duty. So, thought Doyle, the man must have gone before twelve o'clock. What was the best time? People in the hotel often came back from London shows from eleven to eleven thirty. Then the halls were full of people. He could leave without being seen.

If a man wanted to hide himself, why would he leave then? He would not leave to go somewhere else in London, or why would he have come to the hotel at all? He probably wanted to catch a train. Where would he go? Not to a small town. People would be sure to notice him and remember him. Surely he would be going to another big city. So Doyle looked at the time tables for trains. The trains for Edinburgh and Glasgow left around midnight. So, guessed Doyle, he had gone to one or the other of those cities.

Doyle did not always solve such cases as well as Sherlock Holmes did. Once a burglar robbed the village inn near Doyle's home. The village constable and Doyle both tried to catch the man. Doyle again used Holmes' methods. He had decided that the man was left-handed and had nails in his boots. But by that time the constable had already caught the burglar and had thrown him into jail.

Doyle did many other things besides write books. He was a good athlete. He played cricket very well and was a good football player. He learned to box and was runner-up in the amateur billiard championship. In later life he played golf. He made a lecture tour of the United States in 1894. During the Boer War he wrote for an English newspaper. Because of this work he was made a knight and became *Sir* Arthur Conan Doyle. He was interested in the life after death and wrote and talked much about it. He died in 1930.

The Sherlock Holmes stories were read eagerly all over the world. Many people were sure Holmes was a real man and that he really lived in London. Letters came to London addressed to Mr. Sherlock Holmes, 221B Baker Street, for many years. Once some French school boys came to London to visit. They were asked what they wanted to see first. They all cried, "The house where Sherlock Holmes lives!"

During the First World War Doyle went to France. Here he met a French general. The first thing the general asked was what rank Sherlock Holmes had in the British Army. Doyle saw he would never understand that Sherlock Holmes lived only in books. He told the general Holmes was too old to fight.

People have often wanted to put up statues of Sherlock Holmes. A London train has the name "Sherlock Holmes." Many visitors have been to London looking for 221B Baker Street and taking pictures of Baker Street houses.

There are many funny stories about people who tried to use Holmes' methods. One is about the cab driver who was taking Doyle to a hotel in Paris.

"Dr. Doyle," cried the driver, "I see you have been to Constantinople lately. I think you have also been at Barda. You have been near Milan, lately, too."

"Now how could you know that? This is wonderful! Explain."

"I looked at your trunk and saw the city labels there."

Many famous men, especially writers, have loved the Doyle detective stories. They have formed several Sherlock Holmes clubs. Best known are the "Baker Street Irregulars" in New York. Sherlock Holmes sometimes used London boys to do work for him. He called them the Baker Street Irregulars, so the club took that name.

In 1934 the American writer Christopher Morley made up a Sherlock Holmes crossword puzzle for a magazine. The winners were to come to a dinner to honor Holmes. That was the beginning of the club. Others can now get into the club by passing a test on the Holmes stories. The club usually meets on January 6. They have a dinner and talks about the stories. In 1942 one member wrote a song for them called "The Road to Baker Street." Another Holmes club in Boston is "The Speckled Band."

Other Sherlock Holmes Stories

If you like the Sherlock Holmes stories in this book, you may want to read others. You can find all the Sherlock Holmes stories printed together in one or two books and called *The Complete Sherlock Holmes*. There are really four longer stories and five sets of short stories. These are the short stories:

The Adventures of Sherlock Holmes

These are twelve short stories. The first one is "A Scandal in Bohemia," the first Holmes short story.

The Memoirs of Sherlock Holmes

These are eleven short stories. The last one is "The Final Problem," in which Doyle "killed off" Sherlock Holmes and Professor Moriarty.

The Return of Sherlock Holmes

Here are thirteen more short stories. The first one is "The Adventure of the Empty House." This is the story in which Doyle brought Holmes back to life.

His Last Bow

Eight more short stories are found here. Doyle said he tried to retire Sherlock Holmes to a quiet farm in England, but that the first World War made him come back. The eighth story Doyle called "IIis Last Bow," in which Holmes foils a clever German spy.

The Case Book of Sherlock Holmes

These are the last twelve of the fifty-six short stories.

The longer Sherlock Holmes stories are:

A Study in Scarlet

About 135 pages. This is the first Sherlock Holmes tale. Doyle tells how Watson and Holmes met and how they came to live together at 221B Baker Street. In the story Holmes solves a murder case which started among the Mormons in the western United States.

The Sign of the Four

About 100 pages. Holmes uncovers the secrets of hidden treasure and murder, and Watson marries the girl.

The Hound of the Baskervilles

About 170 pages. Sherlock Holmes solves the case of the terrible hound of the Baskerville family and uncovers a murderer's secret.

The Valley of Fear

About 180 pages. Dr. Watson and Holmes solve a mysterious case that began in the United States. Professor Moriarty and Sherlock Holmes begin the struggle that ends at the Reichenbach Fall. This is the least popular of the longer stories.